the SACRED DIARIES

ALSO BY ADRIAN PLASS

Silver Birches: A Novel

The Sacred Diary of Adrian Plass, Aged 37¾

*The Sacred Diary of Adrian Plass,
Christian Speaker, Aged 45¾*

*And Jesus Will Be Born: A Collection of Christmas Poems,
Stories and Reflections*

The Best in Plass

Keeping Up with the Robinsons

You, Me and Mark

Growing Up, Following Jesus

The Sacred Diaries

ENCOUNTERS WITH LEONARD THYNN & ANDROMEDA VEAL

the SACRED DIARIES

Internationally
BESTSELLING AUTHOR
ADRIAN PLASS

ZONDERVAN®

ZONDERVAN.com/
AUTHORTRACKER
follow your favorite authors

We want to hear from you. Please send your comments about this book to us in care of zreview@zondervan.com. Thank you.

ZONDERVAN

The Sacred Diaries
Copyright © 2010 by Adrian Plass

The Horizontal Epistles of Andromeda Veal
Copyright © 1988 by Adrian Plass

The Theatrical Tapes of Leonard Thynn
Copyright © 1994 by Adrian Plass.

Adrian Plass and Dan Donovan assert the moral right to be identified as the author and illustrator of this work.

Requests for information should be addressed to:
Zondervan, Grand Rapids, Michigan 49530

ISBN 978-0-310-29343-9

Cover design: Laura Mason
Interior illustration: Dan Donovan
Interior design: Michelle Espinoza

Printed in the United States of America

10 11 12 13 14 15 /DCI/ 22 21 20 19 18 17 16 15 14 13 12 11 10 9 8 7 6 5 4 3 2 1

CONTENTS

Preface / 7

The Horizontal Epistles of Andromeda Veal / 9

The Theatrical Tapes of Leonard Thynn / 185

PREFACE

Andromeda Veal made her first vociferous appearance in *The Sacred Diary of Adrian Plass, Aged 37 3/4*. Eight years old, and an uncompromising feminist, she took the Plass household in general and Adrian in particular by storm. In church she caused a furore by standing on her chair and singing "She is Lord... !!" at the top of her voice.

In the *Horizontal Epistles* we find Andromeda in a much more troubled and vulnerable state. Having broken her femur she finds herself stranded in hospital on traction – hence her horizontal state. With her mother and father separated, and both away pursuing their particular interests, Andromeda decides to write letters to all sorts of people in the hope that they will write back. These potential correspondents include Margaret Thatcher, God, her mother and father, Charles Cook, a student at Deep Joy Bible School, Adrian Plass, Anne Plass and a monk called Father John who also appeared in the original *Sacred Diary* book. Of the replies she gets, some are ludicrous, some are encouraging, some are funny, some are sad, one or two have very useful things to say to the lonely little girl, and one or two decidedly do not. In the end Andromeda sees the beginnings of hope for the future.

I wrote *Horizontal Epistles* before my one and only daughter was born, and I suspect that part of me was trying to create a little girl all of my own. For this reason, perhaps, the book has always been a favourite of mine.

Leonard Thynn is another *Sacred Diary* original, and possibly the most enigmatic character of all. People often ask me where Leonard came from. Who is he based on? How did you come to create him? Why, in the *Sacred Diary,* was he so anxious to borrow Adrian's cat? The answer to the first two of those questions is that Leonard is based on no one that I ever met, and I have not the faintest idea how he came to be created. He just *was*. Single, probably alcoholic and a decidedly lateral thinker, Thynn lives with his profoundly deaf mother. As well as being a church-member, he has a close friendship with the Plass family, a friendship that borders on dependency for much of the time. Leonard's utterly disastrous attempt to explain the nature of the Trinity by using a carpet sweeper at the front in church as a visual aid (see the *Horizontal Epistles*) has become a thing of legend.

In the *Theatrical Tapes*, Leonard has set himself the task of recording most of the meetings and rehearsals leading up to the performance of a play put on by the church that he attends with Adrian and the others. He records everything, including his mother's inability to understand a single word that is said, and Adrian's intense annoyance with just about all those involved.

Leonard himself is asked to be the prompter, a simple enough request which is seriously complicated by Leonard's mistaken belief that the role requires him to wear a soldier's uniform. Rather than be driven mad by the task of unravelling Thynn's confusion on this point, Adrian agrees...

I suppose it would be true to say that *Theatrical Tapes* revolves around one central joke, which I would be mad to reveal in this introduction. Suffice it to say that a single monumental misunderstanding throws the final performance into a surreal chaos that is relieved only by the unexpectedly positive response of all concerned.

The Theatrical Tapes of Leonard Thynn has been successfully adapted as a play for the stage by a number of groups, both here and in Australia.

THE HORIZONTAL EPISTLES OF ANDROMEDA VEAL

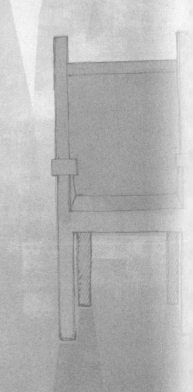

Dear Reader,

A real miracle has happened. Anne and Gerald think I've had a good idea! When I first told them I was going to collect Andromeda's correspondence from the time she was in hospital, they both tutted and clicked their tongues and made sighing noises. Anne said, 'Oh, really darling ...', and Gerald ended up grinning that infuriating grin of his. They thought I was going to get carried away by another of what they call my 'loopy obsessions'. I reminded them that lots of people have been interested enough to read my diary. Anne was gracious enough to nod and say, 'Well, that's true enough, dear,' but Gerald sniggered and said that considering the fact that it was supposed to be a serious book, an awful lot of people had got a lot of laughs out of it. I pointed out that Edwin, our elder, had wept over a number of the entries, but that just set Gerald off cackling to himself, so I didn't say any more at the time.

I'd better explain about Andromeda's letters.

We first met Andromeda (aged seven at the time) when Mrs Veal had to go into hospital, and Edwin, who is Andromeda's uncle, asked if we could put his niece up for a few days. She turned out to be an unusual little girl with a *very* strong personality. We took her to church with us on the Sunday and she caused a sensation to put it mildly! It's all down in my diary (which, despite Gerald's comments, *is* intended to be a sort of spiritual log for the use of future generations, and *not* a religious joke book). Anyway, as I was saying, Andromeda caused quite an impact in church, and also in our family. She adored Anne, she was fascinated by Gerald, and she referred to me as 'The fascist'. She had lots to say about the rights of women, most of it learned from her mother who's a Christian feminist, and she had no qualms about saying it – especially to me! After she'd gone, Anne said she thought there was a lot of worry and tension underneath Andromeda's very grown up way of talking, but I couldn't really see it at the time.

Then, a few months later, Anne got a letter out of the blue from Andromeda, saying that she was on traction in hospital after breaking a femur, and that her parents were not around to visit her. The poor little scrap sounded so lost that Anne decided to mobilise the whole church to help. It was amazing! So many people wrote or visited over the next few weeks. Frank Braddock, our neighbour, wrote a story specially for her, Gerald sent her several letters, Charles Cook sent her two or three rather strange communications from Deep Joy Bible School, and even old Leonard Thynn put pen to paper a couple of times, although the results are – well, read them for yourself! Mrs Flushpool dropped her a line (full of advice and warning of course), and Vernon Rawlings sent her one of his duplicated 'non-begging' letters every now and again. Loads of others wrote, including me – I sent recent extracts from my diary for the times when Andromeda fancied something a little more serious. I'm afraid I couldn't stop Anne's Uncle Ralph from writing. I think his letter is just a bit – well – 'Ralphish'. Still, he meant well. Meanwhile, Andromeda wrote lots of letters herself, some to people in the church, and some to famous people or world leaders, like Cliff Richard and Margaret Thatcher. She never actually sent the 'famous people' ones, but she obviously meant every word!

It was when I was round at Andromeda's house, sometime after she left hospital, that her mum and dad showed me the letters she wrote and never sent, and the ones that people sent to her. I liked them so much that I decided (with Mr and Mrs Veal and Andromeda's permission) to go round all the people in the church and ask for copies of the ones she *did* send. I probably haven't collected them all, but people were very helpful (especially Father John out at the monastery). I think I've got most of them.

When I'd got them all together and in order I showed Anne and Gerald. That's when the miracle happened.

'A good idea!' they said. How about that?

Oh, one more thing – when Andromeda stayed with us, the only thing that would really keep her quiet was Gerald's personal stereo. She got a bit confused though, and always referred to it as his 'Personal problem'. I'm glad I remembered to tell you that.

You might have been a little puzzled by Andromeda's constant references to my son's personal problem!

So there we are. I hope you enjoy reading these letters as much as I enjoyed collecting them.

Yours Truly

Adrian Plass.

PART ONE

PART ONE

Dear Anne,
   I hope you don't mined me writing to you, but I am in trubble. I am an attraction in hospital. Muther has gone to be with the green and common wimmen and I am all aloan. I have fracchered my lemur trying to eat mewsli and rollerskate at the same time. The state have got me horizontall.
  PLEESE WRITE. I am surrounded by impressed wimmen, and plittically unconscious children. Tell the fashist he can write too if he wants only no thacherite claptrap and remember I'm a mizz. Tell Geruld I ~~wouldn't~~ woodn't mined having his persunnel problem to play with while I'm horizontall.
  Anne, who are the green and common wimmen? Muther says they are stopping Prezident Raygun from putting american bottoms in our fields. She has gone with her

frend Gwenda, the one father used to say makes Cyril Smith look anorecksic. Muther was going to stay when they made me an attraction, but Gwenda said love only means you buy a logical bond and the green and common wommen needed her more. Gwenda said lonliness must be fighted. I have fighted it Anne. I think I have lost. Please write to me. I even have to pee horizontall. They left me something to read, but there aren't many pichures in the Soshulist Worker.

Do you know where father lives now Anne? I know he is a laccy of the capitallist pigs but the logical bond he bort for me must have come from a very good shop. He mite come and see me if he heers I'm an attraction.

I have asked God to come and help me, but he hasn't turned up so far.
            PLEESE WRITE!!
            Logical bonds,

                    Andromeda Veal (Mizz)

P. S. If you find out where father
lives, coold you give him a note
for me pleese Anne. It's in the
ennveLlope with this letta.
Thancyou.

Dear daddy,
Please come and see
me or wright to me or fone
me or sumthing, eh?
PLEESE daddy

Logical bonds

Andromeda

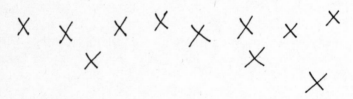

Darling Andromeda,

I've just read your lovely letter. Thanks so much for writing to me. We've *never* forgotten your stay with us. I did three things as soon as I'd read your letter. First, I made a gingerbread man for you and put it in the oven to bake, then I wrapped Gerald's personal stereo up to send with some tapes, and last of all I sat down to write back to you.

You have been in the wars, haven't you? I'd love you to write back and tell me more about the accident and what the doctors said and did. Would you mind doing that?

I think it's American *bases* that Gwenda and mother are protesting about, darling, not *bottoms*. It must have been a very difficult decision for mummy to make, but I'm sure she misses you terribly and will be back soon. I'm afraid I have no idea where your father lives at the moment, but I'm going to ask your Uncle Edwin who, as you know, is the Elder in our church. I've given him your note for daddy as well. I expect he'll come and see you, and so will I soon. You must be *so* uncomfortable, you poor love. The other thing I've done is to write down a list of lots of names and addresses of people in our church, and I've sent you plenty of paper and envelopes and stamps so that you can write to them. I'll get Uncle Edwin to tell everybody you're going to write and I'm sure you'll get loads and loads of replies. I've told Uncle Adrian (whom you quite rightly describe as 'the fascist') to send you some extracts from his diary from time to time, and Gerald promises to write too.

Be brave, sweetheart! Remember Jesus loves all little children, and he's already turned up without you knowing it. See you soon.

Love, Anne.

XXX

Dear Anne,

I cryed a bit when your parsel came. Mother's frend Gwenda says tears are a sign of weekness, but its hard to be strong when you are horizontall, Anne. You mustn't call them gingerbread men by the way. Muther made me a gingerbread <u>person</u> wonce. She said the men sort are sexist. Yours tastes just the same though. I hope there are no harmfull addititives in it. Gwenda says that bad temper and murder and rape and war are all caused by harmful addititives. She and muther said they were going to only live on grapes once because all the other food was full of harmful addititives. Gwenda said that in a few days they would be tall and strong and clean. By the third day they were crauling round the kitchen floor pewking up bits of grape. I stuck to having mewsli every day. It is a bit like eating your way out of a haystak, but at least you don't pewk up. Father used to annoy Gwenda when he was still living at home by saying he wanted a nice fat E102 sandwich for tea. I don't think father liked Gwenda. I hope Uncle Edwin finds father soon, Anne. My logical bond hurts.

It was orful when I broke my lemur, Anne! Muther said I had fifteen seconds to get my rollerskates off, eat my mewsli and get reddy for bed. I tried to do them all at once and fell down. When we got to the hospital a man looked at my leg and said he was the sturgeon who was going to mend me. He said he was called <u>Mister</u> Fisher. Just my luck to get an uncwollified one! He said I'd got to be an attraction for weeks and weeks, so here I am. Oh, Anne, it's a real pain in the base!

Thanks for the persunnel problem and all the stuff. Are you sure Jesus has turned up?

Logical bonds

Andromeda.

P.S. Do you think you've got just a
bit of a logical bond for me, Anne?
Do you think you mite have?

Dear Andromeda,

Anne Plass has just phoned me to say you've had a bit of a disaster! You really do things in a big way, don't you my adorable little niece. I wish Mum had let me know before she went, but never mind – we'll cope. Anne says she's sending you lots of stationery, and I'm going to let everyone in the church know that letters would be appreciated. No point being an Elder if you can't use it sometimes, eh, cherub? I'll be along to see you of course, and I'm sure there'll be a few others coming to stare at the only Veal in captivity! By the way, why not drop a few lines to some of our world leaders? You never know, you might change the history of the world!

As far as getting in touch with your dad is concerned, I'll do my very best, but, as you know, he did leave home rather suddenly, and so far no one I've asked seems to know where he's got to. Don't worry though – he's bound to get in touch eventually. He's always been quite crackers about you, Andromeda, you know that. We'll all be praying for you, love. See you soon.

Best wishes,

Uncle Edwin.

P.S. Don't give the nurses too hard a time, honey. They're not used to political activists like you!

The Gremlin,
Red Square,
Moscow,
Russia.

Dear Mister Gorgeouschops,
You don't know me, but I am a
small english soshulist called Mizz
Veal — Mizz Andromeda Veal. I am
eight and I am an attraction in
hospital. Pleese don't think you've
got to stop your breckfast in the
Gremlin kitchen just to read my
letter. I know you are very bizzy
and ockupied in Affganistan and
trying to get the pollit-bureau open
and stopping Prezident Raygun from
watching Star Wars on the moon,
but I wanted to ask you sumthing.
Everyone says you are not like Linen
and Starling and the bald thick one
who fighted with tables at the Untied
Nations. The thing is — I was wun-
dering if I could be your speshul
adviser when I am bigger. I can't
do much at the moment because
the state have got me horizontall

til the bones nit, but I am a soshulist like you and I could help. I
know ruffly where Margaret Thacher
lives, so I could show your G.B.H.
agents which tube to get off at if
they wanted to infiltraight her whe-
n the reverlooshun comes. Also I
could warn you when birds fly over-
head so you don't get those nasty
splodges all over your head! Your
Russian pigeons must be a size Mister
Gorgeouschops!

One thing I don't like is your
camps. They don't sound much fun.
Mother read to me about one in a book
called A day in the life of Ivan
Something that sounds like a sneeze,
but I think Starling was Akela at
that one so I'll let you off.

By the way my frend Geruld
(we share his persunnel problem) told
me that Neil Kinnock is an anagram
of I knock Lenin. Puts you off a
bit, eh?

Logical bonds,
Andromeda Veal (Mizz)
P.S. Don't tell muther I wrote will

you? She says Russian soshulism is a load of crab, but I think you look nice.

P. P. S. We've got one of yours over here already. He's in charge of lots of minors and he's got two brillo pads stuck to his head. His name is sumthing like Half a lagers brill.

P.P.P.S. Have you ever had to pee horizontall while you've been in charge of Russia?

Dear Andromeda,

Name of Thynn. Leonard Thynn. Friend of the Plasses – well, think I'm a friend. *Am* a friend. Sure of it! Friend of the Plasses. Adrian: tall, friendly, simple type. Anne: sweet, lovely, wonderful. Gerald: good lad, speaks his mind, not everyone likes what's *in* his mind. I do. Took me home and helped me to bed once when I got a bit – tired. Yes, definitely a friend of the Plasses. They certainly like *me* – well, they seem to. Quite often borrow their cat for – never mind what for. Used to have some pets myself. Cat called Brandy. Budgie called Soda. Two goldfish called Ice and Lemon. Funny eh? No, not really. Bit of a give-away actually. Got a little problem – well, not a *little* problem, more of a *big* problem, with thingy. Drink. Too much, that is. Yes.

Anyway – 'nough about the wretched Thynn. About you, young Veal! Hear you came a cropper. Bust your whatnot. In for running repairs, eh, girl? Well – not *running* repairs. Silly word to use really. More like 'hanging about' repairs. Femur I'm told. Fearfully fiddly fings femurs. Bit of a joke there. Well, not quite a joke, more of a – well, bit silly really. Always rather enjoyed alliteration. That's when all the first letters are – sorry! Drivelling on rather. Habit of mine.

Look! Thought I'd tell you a funny story. Cheer you up a bit. Not very good at it, but I'll have a go. Starts after the next full stop. This chap – walking through a forest. (Doesn't have to be a forest, you understand. Could be a wood, copse, clump – any sort of arboreal assembly, as long as trees are in the picture. Got it? Good.) Well, this chap is walking (or he could be strolling or ambling. Not striding. Striding spoils the story), he's walking, strolling or ambling through this forest, copse, wood or clump, when all of a sudden he notices a little chap (not abnormally little, I don't mean, more sort of at the bottom end of the 'not a dwarf' range), and this comparatively little chap is squatting behind a tree. I expect you're saying to yourself, 'How did the chap (the one walking through the forest, copse, etc... .) notice the little chap at all (the squatter, that is) if he was behind a tree?' Well, the answer is that the squatter, vertically deficient though he might have been, was significantly broader (in the squatting posture at any rate) than the tree behind which he squatted. Clear? Good.

So, then the strolling chap calls out to the squatting chap (and we're getting a lot closer to the funny bit now), he calls out, 'Hello!'. Then the squatting chap – presumably craning his neck round his tree to see the strolling chap – (actually, he's probably not strolling any more – probably stopped just before addressing the squatting chap, but I'll go on calling him the strolling chap so as not to confuse you. Okay?) – now where was I? Oh, yes, the squatting chap calls over to the strolling chap and says, 'Hello!' back. Then, the strolling chap, who obviously doesn't have even a passing acquaintanceship with the smallish squatter, says, 'What are you?', and the chap replies, 'I'm a tinker.' Then the stroller says (and this really is the final bend before hitting the old punchline – *ever* so funny! Well, *I* think it's funny – well, *quite* funny), he says, 'What are you doing squatting behind that tree?' And the chap answers (I'll put it on a separate line because this is IT, the joke proper), he says:

'I'm tinking.'

Get it? I'm *tinking*. What are you doing? I'm *tinking*. Good 'un, eh? Hope it's not a bit too – you know, bit too thingy.

Anyway, sorry about the leg and – the leg. Told mother I wanted to write to Andromeda. Poor old Mum. Deaf as a post. Said if I wanted to bite a chronometer I must be even loonier than she'd thought. Still – sent her love when she understood. Said a prayer with her about you last night. God's alright. Doesn't give up, not with me anyway. Do slip sometimes. Doesn't give up. I could tell you some stories – anyway.

Regards,

Thynn (Leonard).

P.S. Do hope the funny story was, well – you know.

Deep Joy Bible School
Narrowpath Road
Dumpton
Wessex.

Greetings in the name of one who is strong and mighty in deed
and word to usward – able to give and provide from his marvellous bounty more than the simple heart of man can imagine,
to bring salvation and eternal life through the outpouring of his
boundless love to we who, in the latter years, were lost in sin and
death, and through his great and immeasurable love to bring us
at last safely to heaven's shore through the storm-tossed waves
of that sea of life, the crossing of which is the portion of all men
until we are called in the fullness of time, and on a day that was
appointed and fixed before time began, to be with him for all
eternity in the distant and shining place where all is peace and
contentment because he is there and prepares a dwelling for us
that we might also, undeserving though we be, inherit a kingdom
of everlasting joy – from one saved and brought to repentance
by that same grace from the sinful and rebelliously hard-hearted
nature which all men since Adam have most shamefully endured,
and brought finally after tribulation and the ministry of the saints
to the knowledge of joy in-working through his soul, by the
matchless and powerful movement of that heavenly will in one
who shall throughout all ages be deeply thankful for that wonderful beneficence, and awaits with humble obedience the call that
will herald his translation into Paradise – to a sister and partaker
in the mystical body wherein we all share, who, caught up in the
blessed mystery of saving power is one with the saints and martyrs
now and through the life hereafter –

Dear Andromeda,

No time to write more now. Will write again soon.

Love, Charles.

Dear Andromeda,

Uncle Ralph here – Anne's uncle really, but I could be yours as well if you like. Anne said you were in for a stretch (Gettit! Stretch! Traction!), so I said I'd write and cheer you up with a few of me jokes. Rib-ticklin' Ralph they call me at work (among other things! Know what I mean?). I went to hospital once with a pain in the neck, but she left after I'd settled in. Eh? Anne said leave the jokes out, but you need a laugh, don't you? Pretty little nurse looked after me when I was in. She said, 'I'm just going to give you a little injection Mr Surtees, I hope it won't put you off me.' I said, 'You couldn't give me the needle if you tried, Nurse!' Laugh! I nearly asked for a bottle. They were a good bunch those nurses, though. Loads of patience. Mind you, they'd have nothing to do if they hadn't got any patients, would they? (Gottit? Patience – patients. Eh?). Doctors were a bit of a miserable lot. I said to one, 'Look, doc, I've had three different bits of me taken out in the last five years. You sure you haven't got a deal on with the local take-away?' Didn't even smile. He must have been foreign. The ward sister was a bit of a gloom and doom merchant too. Tried me best to cheer her up. I'd smuggled this bottle of imitation blood in, see? So one day after I'd asked for the bed pan and they'd put the old curtains round, I tipped it all down me chin and me chest, and hung over the side of the bed with me tongue lolling out and me eyes all wide and staring. Did she bite! I'll say she did! Panic! Emergency! Did she swing into action, or did she swing into action! Then, when she lifted me back on the bed, I grinned at her and said, 'I've finished with the bed pan, Sister.' I've never seen anyone so angry. She got her revenge though. Won't tell you how – let's just say that with friends like her, who needs enemas? Eh? I think the Italians call 'em innuendoes. With me?

I'm coming your way soon, so I'll drop in and say hello. Don't do anything I wouldn't do!

Cheers

Uncle Ralph.

P.S. What's the difference between a nurse with something in her eye, and a boil that's getting better? Answer – one's a blinking sister, and the other's a sinking blister. Gettit? Good 'un, eh?

Dear Anne,

Thankyou verry mutch for arsking yor Uncle Ralf to rite me a letta. It wos a bit of a funnee letta tho Anne. He said he was going to put lots of jokes in to chear me up, but I coodun't find a singul one! Still, he sounds nice and happee.

Anne, I think I mite write to Geruld if that's orlright. Muther said he sounded like one of the plitical corpsis yew see warking about aul the thyme but he was very frendly when I staid with you eeven tho he took the micky owt of me and said that FEMINIST is a nammagranam of I FIST MEN, and wen I said I diddun't thinc that wos verry funny he ticcled me and maid me larf, and woodun't stop untill I said — Corrunashun Street is maud in Personchester — three thymes. There hasn't bean mutch larfing in our house lately, Anne. Muther's frend Gwenda said

34

that wen the reverlooshun cums,
jokes will be judged on hou fare
they are to minpor;ty groops, and
farther said - are yew seeriously
saying that joaks doon't have to bee
funnee ? - and Gwenda said - that's
rite - and farther said - in that
cayse Bob Munkhowse must be the
Chay Gavara of commedy - and
muther put his pipe terbacco in the
food mixa with sum jelly.
   Oh, Anne, I carn't tell yew what
it's lyke to be stretched owt withowt
a pairent. I wood eeven tork to a
raiving fashist antee-reverlooshun-
ery if they wood be kined to me lyke
a pairent, but doon't tell ennyone
I said that, or Kneel Kinnerk
will nevver let me cum to his partee. Who do yew vote four, Anne?
I think yew shood be the leada of
the NICE partee, I do. Cum and
sea me soon, eh?
                    Logical Bonds
                    Andromeda.

P.S. Geruld's not ingaged or enny of that, is he?

Dear Andromeda,

I was so sorry to hear about your fractured lemur – I mean femur. Gerald asked me to say that he hopes that you don't end up with one leg shorter than the other. He said if you do, *he* can't do anything about it, but he knows a man who can. I think he's going to write to you soon. Now that *will* be a miracle!

Anyway – Auntie Anne says she thinks you might want to read an extract from my diary. I can't think why. It is, after all, a serious document. I hope it's not too 'fashist' for you ...

Thursday

Read a great article in a magazine called 'Jam for 21st Century Christian Families Who Don't Buzz Any More'. All about enjoying God's natural creation. Decided a good old family ramble was called for. Anne agreed. Gerald, in one of his cynical moods, said he was fed up with 'rambles, quiche, light jokes, cherryade, harmless fun, and all the other pseudo-Christian baggage that gets dragged around the church'. Got cross with him and insisted he comes on Saturday.

Prayed hard tonight for good weather at the weekend.

Friday

Distinctly overheard Gerald praying for rain as I passed his bedroom this morning. Locked myself in the bathroom and prayed for sunshine again.

We shall see!!

Rang Richard Cook and invited him along too. Gerald said he'd only come if he could bring a new girlfriend called Noreen, who's not a Christian. Agreed rather doubtfully. Hope she gets on alright with Richard. He is such a *Christian* Christian.

Saturday

Woke to brilliant sunshine. Tried not to look smug over my cornflakes. Gerald very glum.

Set off, all in our car, at 10.30 am. Absolute cloudburst the instant I switched the engine on. Ignored Gerald clapping in the back and carried on anyway.

Poor old Richard Cook was jammed in the back between Noreen, Gerald's girlfriend, who turns out to be a very large girl, and Noreen's pet, Paws, who is a huge black hairy dog.

After a while Richard said, in a muffled voice, 'Is your mansion booked in Paradise, Noreen?'

Noreen stopped putting on her bright pink lipstick for a moment, and said, 'No, love, we're just 'avin' days out this year. Can't afford to go away.'

Richard told her he'd meant was she a Christian, and added that he was a charismatic. 'You know what that means do you, Noreen?' he asked.

Noreen said she did because she'd had an uncle who had to stick this thing up his nose whenever his tubes got blocked.

' 'Ere!' she went on, 'You're not one o' them mormons are you?'

'Certainly not!' said Richard through a mouthful of Paws. 'I abhor sects!'

'Not much fun for your wife then,' said Noreen dispassionately.

Blank silence.

Richard said, 'What a charming dog, Noreen.'

'Y-e-e-e-s,' said Noreen affectionately. 'Say hello to Uncle Dickie-doos, Pawsy-poos.'

'Oh dear,' said Gerald a moment later, 'Pawsy-poos has sicky-pood all over Uncle Dickie-doo's shoesy-woos.'

Stopped and let Richard out to clean his shoes with handfuls of grass. Sun came out immediately. Put Richard back next to the window beside Gerald. Stopped a mile later when Gerald was sick all over Richard's shoulder because of the smell.

Nobody hungry when we got to the picnic site. Everything smelled of dog vomit. Paws stole a ham and a huge trifle from the picnic basket while no one was watching. Richard went white and asked if there was a bus back to town.

Went for a short walk but had to dash back when the rain started. Richard begged pathetically to be allowed to sit in front. Anne sat next to wet Paws, who wasn't sick once on the journey back.

Arrived home and all got out of the car. Fine rain and sunshine at the same time.

'Ooh, look!' said Noreen pointing upwards.

We all looked. It was a beautiful rainbow.

Gerald and I smiled at each other.

Anne nodded wisely.

Paws brought up the trifle.

Richard said, 'I know I am not renowned for verbal flippancy, but were you aware that "God's creation" is an anagram of "Dog's reaction"?'

See you soon,

Love, Uncle Adrian.

P.S. I do hope we end up friends despite our political differences.

Dear Geruld,

I eggspect your muther has told you I am a horizontall attraction at the moment what with the lemur nitting and everything. I play with your persunnel problem all the time so I don't hear much, except when your Uncle Ralf vizited me and he pinched Nurse Roundway's base and she screemed so loud I heard it right through the beejees. I like Nurse Roundway. She smiles like a apple. I thort she'd report Uncle Ralf to the sturgeon, but after he'd gone she arsked if he was coming again. Tell you what though, Geruld — sh'es got a loony family. Last night she arsked me if I wanted sumthing to read so I told her I'd got a Soshulist Worker and muther doesn't let me read chilldren's books becouse they poison the mined, speshully Eden Blighted, the one who farther told me writes the Newrotic Nine books.

Gwenda said that Goldiloks and the three bears should really be called Arkytipal woman despretlly struggles to snatch a few crumms back from three vicious myth-images of male dommination.

Anway, Nurse Roundway said (yor not going to beleeve this Geruld) she said that her little neece who is the same age as me, won't go to sleep unless she's bin able to cuddle up with her <u>poo</u>. I know it takes all soughts, Geruld, but that strikes me as dissgussting, and I thort we were talking about books anyway.

The fashist you live with sent me a bit of his dairy. I liked it. I liked Paws. I've never had a pet, Geruld. Father was going to get a dog wonce, but muther woodn't let him because she arsked him what he rearly thought of Gwenda, and he said "Clothes by Billy Smart and perfume by paranoya." I've never had a dolly either, Geruld. Muther says they are sosieties tool for reeinforsing the subjektiv female roll, but Gwenda said I could have a little plastic man I saw in a toyshop as long as I cauled it Bigot. I luvved Bigot, Geruld, but he got broke when muther threw him at father after she said that Gwenda fild a big space in her life and father said it must be a blinking grate gap if Gwenda fild it.

Pleese come and see me Geruld and tell the fashist I woodn't mined a bit more dairy. Pleese pray that muther will come back from the green and common wimmen soon.

All my logical bonds,
Andromeda

P.S. Did you notiss the bit where I said I havn't got a dolly, Geruld? They are bad things but it woodn't be my fawlt if sumone gived me one wood it?

P.P.S. Eh?

Cosmos Evangelism Outreach
Universal Conversion College Project
Prefab Number 3
Armistice Row
Bagshot

Telephone (Bill awaits faith income)

Dear Brother or Sister,

Please excuse the faint print and poor quality paper of our
newsletter but funds are low as we enter the ninety-eighth phase
of our project to build the Universal Conversion College. As you
know from our previous letter we are aiming for a total sum of
23.5 million pounds. At present we have just topped the thirteen pounds fifty pence mark and it is marvellous to see the work
grow. Only last week one of us found five pence in the precinct,
and we have also had a number of Tizer bottles donated which
should realise a return substantially close to the sum of thirty
pence. It is a great encouragement when you are living by faith as
we are, to see how all that is needful is provided. We eat regularly
(it is my turn to eat on Tuesdays and Thursdays) and it is amazing how many games and activities can be successfully organised
in the dark. It occurred to me last night, as I lay trying to sleep
on the linoleum, that our policy of never asking for financial support is what separates us out from those projects which seem to
be constantly begging. The space provided at the bottom of this
letter for Barclaycard numbers is purely intended for those who
feel personally led to share their wealth and comfort with brothers and sisters fighting a lonely battle on the rugged frontiers of
Christian endeavour.

Some have queried the fact that one of our original prophetic
words to the effect that the college would be built and the whole
of England and Wales converted by last Wednesday, has fallen a
little short of fulfilment. We now feel led to say, however, that we
believe this to be due to a spirit of meanness in some individual
outside the project. We prayed for him or her last night as we read

the story of Ananias and Sapphira by candlelight. Do you know that story, friend?

Yours,

Vernon Rawlings (sic sec)

P.S. We are also anxious that you should not leave large sums of money to the college in your will, unless you are absolutely sure that you wish to support the Lord's work, rather than leave the money to people who are already comfortably off.

P.P.S. We are studying the book of James at present. What a fine message it presents!

PART TWO

PART TWO

Dear Anne,

Muther rung me up this mourning from a place near the green and common wimmen. It was a very bad line. I arsked her if Mister ~~Raygun~~ had bin for his base yet, but she said there are still a lots of crude rissoles behind a fence, so she can't come back yet. She said she cryed last night when she thought of me being an attraction and horizontall, but Gwenda said it was just a bad cayse of G.M.T., and G.M.T. always makes wimmen tense. I arsked Nurse Roundway what G.M.T. means. She said it means Grennich Mean Time. Why does Grennich Mean Time always make wimmen tense, Anne? Are we all going looney or what?

A man in a backwoods collar came round today Anne. I was the only one he spoke to. He said he was ~~cauld~~ cauled the Neverend Boom, and it was his first time in the hospital. Just before he went I arsked him why he hadn't spoken to ennyone else. He said it was because I was the only one with P for Prottistant at the end of my bed. He said all the others had R.C. for Roaming Catlicks, C.F. for Christian Felloaship, or B. for Baptists or S.A. for Salvation Army. He'd gonn before I cood tell him. P. is for Porridge and R.C. is for Rice Crispies, and C.F. is for Corn Flakes, and B. is for Bran, and S.A. is for Stewed Apple. I thort I was the stupiddist person in the world, Anne, but Neverend Boom wins by a mile.

Did Geruld notiss the bit in my letter where I said I havn't got a dolly, Anne? Because I havn't got one of those bad things. If he gets me one I won't upset him by not taking it. I will pretend I like it.

Logical bonds
Andromeda

P.S. If Jesus only likes good little

girls, I don't think he will like me,
Anne. I am affrayed I was pleased
when muther said she cryed.
Yes I was, Anne.

Darling Andromeda,

Just a quick note to say that there's one address I didn't give you that I meant to. Do you remember, sweetheart, when you stayed with us, you met Father John? He was dressed in a long brown cloak and he was going rather bald on top. Now I come to think about it, you didn't actually *meet* him, but you saw him in the next door garden talking to Frank Braddock, our neighbour. Father John is a very kind, wise man, and I know he'd be only too happy to help with any problems you might have. Do write to him if you want to, darling. The address is on the back of this letter. See you soon.

Love Anne

X X X

Hey, Andy Pandy! Gerald here!

What's going on? I hear you lost a battle with a stone floor and now you're on the rack down at St Whatsit's. Thanks for your letter by the way. Best letter I ever had, especially the bit about old Uncle Ralph giving your Nurse Roundway a tweak. Sounds as if he's well in there! Like the bit about 'Eden Blighted – the one who wrote the Neurotic Nine books' as well. Something tells me I'd get on really well with your father – which reminds me, I'm not one of your get-up-at-dawn-and-pray-for-three-hours types, but I have been flicking the odd tiddly-wink up towards Holy Head Office. So have lots of others, so we'll probably see a bit of action in that area before long. Get in touch with old Father John – pure gold, he is. Talking about fathers – dear old Dad (the fascist, you know) is his same old loony self. Dad's pure gold in his own way as well, but he does get himself into some scrapes. The other day my cousin Wanda rang to ask if we could look after her babies for one night. Oh, Andy Pandy, you should see 'em! Triplets – three boys, one year old, and their names are Shadrach, Meshach, and Abednego. Their dad's a Christian steelworker, so he's really into fiery furnaces. Anyway, Mum was out when the call came, so Dad took it, and his end of the chat went something like this.

'Hello, Wanda ... yes, I see ... yes, I understand ... yes of course it's an emergency, I can see that ... just for the Friday night? ... oh, yes! No problem ... of course I mean it. We adore children ... no it's not Wanda, it's nothing at all. You just go ahead and make the arrangements and don't even think about Friday night ... no, it's a pleasure *really*. I'll enjoy it ... Yes ... 'bye Wanda.'

All through the call I was trying to attract Dad's attention, Andy, but he kept waving me away like he does when he gets exasperated. So after he'd put the phone down he turned to me and started ticking me off.

'I should have thought,' he said, all dignified, 'that it might be possible to speak on the telephone in my own house' (he only owns about one brick, Andy) 'without my son waving like a dervish at me because he can't wait to make some totally irrelevant comment!'

'Sorry, Dad,' I said, 'I was just trying to tell you that ...'

Mum came through the door just then and asked what was going on. So Dad explained, still very dignified, and when he got to the bit about me trying to interrupt, she just leaned back against the door and started giggling.

'I wasn't aware,' said Dad, 'that anything I've said is particularly amusing.'

'No, it's not really, darling,' said Mum, 'it's just that I think what Gerald was trying to say to you was that I'm not actually here on Friday night, am I? Remember? I promised I'd stay with Samantha Rind-Smythe for the night, didn't I, sweetheart?'

Poor old Dad went all white and quivery, Andy, and he made a little screaming sound in his throat. He tried to 'unfix' it with Wanda, but she wasn't in when he phoned back, and he knew she'd have made all her arrangements by the time he could get in touch with her.

So there we were Friday evening, Mum away till the next morning, and Dad, wild-eyed but determined, doing a real Forth Bridge job on Shadrach, Meshach and Abednego. I think Dad was actually getting to quite like them after a while, except for Abednego perhaps. Abednego really does look incredibly like Bernard Manning, Andy, and his sense of humour isn't much different. He threw his jelly and cream all over Dad, then laughed and clapped.

Anyway, by ten o'clock Shadrach and Abednego were asleep, but Meshach had decided he wanted a long and important chat with Dad. He waved his little arms around and babbled away for ages (just like some of the people in our church), and Dad sat, a bit pop-eyed with tiredness, and listened to him.

'Do you think he's really saying something?' asked Dad after a while.

'Yes,' I said, 'I think he's trying to give you a message – something from scripture, I expect. In fact, I think I can interpret what he's saying.'

Old Dad's just a little bit easy to play jokes on, Andy Pandy. I got a piece of paper, wrote on it, put it in an envelope, sealed it up and handed it to Dad.

'Here you are, Dad,' I said, 'this is the verse I think he's trying to say to you. You open it in the morning and I bet you find it's an accurate prophecy.'

Dad said tiredly, 'Don't be silly, Gerald', but he put the envelope in his pocket, and I went off to bed.

You should have seen Dad when I came down the next morning, Andy. He looked like a dead walrus. Shadrach, Meshach and Abednego were cackling and chattering and crawling and dribbling all over him.

'Good night, Dad?' I said.

Poor old Dad was just a grey lump with a grey voice.

'No, Gerald,' he said faintly, 'I did not have a good night. I had a very bad night. I had an awful, dreadful, appalling night. Meshach continued to talk to me for the entire night, his conversation interrupted only by two dirty nappies. Shadrach had a wet nappy at one o'clock and needed a bottle at three-thirty, and Abednego had two dirty nappies, three wet ones and a screaming fit. They have *all* been awake since five o'clock and if you make any jokes I am going to kill you.'

'Of course I won't make any jokes, Dad,' I said soothingly, 'but aren't you going to look at Meshach's prophecy?'

Dad looked at me with narrowed, bleary eyes for a moment, then dragged the envelope from his pocket and tore it open.

'Go on, Dad,' I said, 'read out what Meshach was trying to say to you last night.'

Dad screwed his eyes up, then read out loud.

'One Corinthians: chapter fifteen, verse fifty-one: We shall not all sleep, but we shall all be changed.'

Had to get out quick then, Andy Pandy, or he'd have thrown Abednego at me. I took pity on Dad after that actually. Sent him

53

back to bed and wrestled with the terrible trio till Mum got home. Do you think he'll put it all in his precious diary? I bet he does!

Anyway, my little stretched friend, that's all for now. I'll be along later in the week, and I'm afraid I *have* bought you a dolly. I hope you don't mind.

Love, Gerald.

P.S. I've got a puzzle for you! Whose name is this an anagram of?

'LOVE AND A DREAM'

P.P.S. An anagram is when you mix the letters up, but I expect you know that, you clever girl.

Dear Geruld,
        I have werked it owt.
Love and a dream is an dnnnagr-
amm of Adam Ovalender!

        L. B's
        Andromeda

Dear Andy Pandy,

Good try – Wrong! Try again …

Love, Gerald.

Dear Farther John,

　　I know you are a halibut nunk, but is it aul right for small girls with broke lemurs who are attractions in hosspittall to write to you? Do you live in a nunkery? Are you aloud to talk? If you aren't you ort to get a personnel problem like my frend Geruld. They don't harf pass the time if you're horizontall or not aloud to talk. I was going to be a none wonce, but farther laughed and said I'd never get into the habit. Why is that funny? I am only a small size.

　　Ennyway, I've got some cwestions to ask you abowt God and things. Gwenda said that relijun is the opeeum of the masses, and farther said is that why Roaming Catlicks look so glassy-eyed in church? Muther used to say prairs with me, but lately Gwenda's read me bits by sumone cauled Mouse A. Tongue at bedtime from sumthing cauled the little read book. I'm not surprised it's a little read book, Father John. I'd have more fun cuddling up with my poo like Nurse Roundway's dissgusting little neece.

Anne Plass says Jesus is allready here but I am not so shore unless he's dissgised as Mister Blogg, the porter. I hope not. Mister Blogg is a very windy person and spits in those little paper bags on the wall when Nurse Roundway's not looking. I wood be a bit dissappointid if that turned out to be Jesus, woodn't you Farther John?

Here are my cwestions.

Who made God?

Where is God?

Where is hevven?

Why didn't he stop my lemur braking?

Why dussn't he bring muther back from the green and common wimmen when I arsk him?

Where is farther?

Why dussn't he bring him when I arsk?

Can I have some chocklit soon?
Will Germain Greer get in?

What was the R101? (Farther said Gwenda made it look like a chippolarter and she was a much greater disarster).

When will I stop being an attraction?

Do you still go to hevven if yor glad your muther cried? (Don't tell God I arsked that one for goodness sake!)

Logical bonds to aul in
the Nunkery,

Andromeda Veal

P.S. Is the cheef nunk cauled a costello?

My dear Mizz Veal (may I call you Andromeda?),

I can honestly say that I have never enjoyed reading a letter more than I enjoyed reading yours. I took it into breakfast with me and laid it beside my boiled egg so that I could enjoy it in peace. We are not allowed to speak at breakfast, so I nearly got told off by the chief nunk (who certainly ought to be called a Costello, even if he isn't), because I kept chuckling over the wonderful things you wrote. We halibut nunks need all the smiles we can get, so I am very grateful to you. Life at the nunkery can be a little quiet at times, although the other brothers are all very nice. By the way, dear Anne Plass did telephone me a few days ago to say that you were in hospital after a nasty accident, so I was planning to come and see you at the same time as I visit my cousin Pearl, who has just had a little baby called George. Would you like me to bring George to see you when I come? As I expect you know, we halibuts don't usually do much marrying and having babies, so I would just love to come and show George off to you as if he were my very own, instead of being a beloved little nephew. Please let me do that.

Now, as to your questions – oh, Andromeda! I felt quite frightened. Such good questions, and so many of them! We nunks are supposed to know all about these things, but I just sat shaking my head and feeling silly. Then Brother Wilf, who is very old with two little tufts of white sticking-up hair, asked me what was the matter. I said that a young friend had written to ask me some very difficult questions about God, and I wasn't sure of the answers.

'Down to the lake, Brother John!' he said. 'Walk down to the lake and see what you find. I will attend to your duties. Away with you!'

One day, Andromeda, Brother Wilf will turn into a bright smile and just float away to heaven.

Down to the lake I went, to see what I would find. I do hope you will be able to see the lake near our nunkery when your leg is better, Andromeda. It is a shining, peaceful thing surrounded by all sorts of trees, and there is a soft quiet path running all the way round so that you can walk and walk until you come back to the place where you started. Here is a secret, Andromeda – just between you and I – sometimes I *skip* along that path. Yes! Can you imagine it – me, in my long brown habit, skipping along like some silly old sheep who's forgotten he's not a lamb any more?

Anyway, I walked along for a bit, listening to all those tiny lapping sounds you hear near lakes, until I came to one of my special places where an old wooden platform pushes out through the reeds into clear water. I stood right at the edge of the jetty, folded my arms in the big sleeves of my cloak and had a little conversation with God. I've put down what we said as though it was a sort of play. FJ is me by the way, Andromeda.

FJ:(Trying to feel holy and good) God, I have some questions ...

GOD: (Interrupting) Look at that little coot among the reeds, John. Look at his little white face. I expect he's looking for some food. I made him, you know. What do you think?

FJ:Very nice, God – very nice, but these questions.

GOD: (Interrupting again excitedly) John! John! Look what's coming down the bank towards us. It's Mother Goose with her old man and all the kids. Look how she's nagging away at them from the back. Aren't you glad you're a halibut? Look how the fluffy children are marching along in line minding their P's and Q's. Dad's got his head down, John. He's having a hiss at you, warning you not to start any aggro. Better not start any aggro, John. No joke, a goose peck. Oh, those babies are so pretty! Not bad, eh, John?

FJ:*Very* attractive, God. Very nice, but ...

GOD: (Sounding a little sad) Oh, John, you should have seen it in the beginning! It was so lovely. It will be again one day too. That's exciting isn't it, John? Isn't it?

FJ:It's very exciting, God, of course it is. God, about Andromeda ...

GOD: (He does interrupt, doesn't he?) John, have you ever made a goose?

FJ: Err ... no, God.

GOD: Have you ever built a coot, John?

FJ: No, God, I've never built a coot.

GOD: Well, let *me* tell *you* that making coots and geese is very complicated. Helping Andromeda is a piece of cake compared with building a coot. You go and tell her I love her very much, and she'll get all her answers as time goes by. I'm working on it right now. You will tell her, won't you, John?

FJ: Yes, God, I will tell her.

Look out for me and George, Andromeda. You should be able to tell us apart. We're both bald, but he dribbles more than me.

God bless from all at the nunkery,

Father John.

P.S. Why don't you write a letter to God? I do sometimes.

Dear Geruld,
          Gott it! It's Mad Ronald
Eave.
                    L. B's

                         Andromeda

Dear Andromeda,

Wrong again! Here's a clue. Love and a dream is an anagram of the name of someone I like very much. Good luck!

Love, Gerald.

Dear Mister Pluckley-Turf,

I got yor name from somone in the hospittal where I am a long-term attraction since the old lemur bitt the dust. Being horizontall doesn't mean you carn't have vertic-kal opinions you gnow, and seeing as you are our local ~~repri~~ ~~repp~~ ~~repree~~ ~~repperez~~ m. p. I thort I'd write you a greevance about the Natural Health Surface in jenerdl and this hosspitall in paticular. My frend Gerald (he has kindley donated his persunnel problem for hosspittal use) says that even though I am a left-leaning red person and you are a blue Thacher-scratcher, you still have to lissen to me becos I'm one of your constitititituents. I may be onley eight now, but in ten yeers I shall be aloud to vote, eh, Pluckley-Turf, old man? If you want to be a miniskirt of health and soshul obscuritee one day you'll need all the votes you can gett!

Ennyway! It's about Nurse Roundway who looks arfter me. She is very
round and kined and smiles a lot,
but the uther day she was crying in
the nite when she thort I was
asleep, and I arsked why and she
jumped like a ambushed beachball
and told me it was becos she is
verry tired becos there is lots to do
and not enough nurses to do it and
she tries to do more but carn't
and she's sad becos peeple arn't
getting lookt after like thay
should. Then she made a beamy
smile come on her face and said
she was being silly and making a
fuss like a stewpid old woman and she
playd three littal words with me til
I dropt off.

All you've got to do, Mister Plu-
ckley - Turf is stand up in the
House of Comments and say that
Nurse Roundway cried and then
everyone will undastand and Mrs.
Thacher will tell the civil serpents
to give all the hospittalls some
more money and all the Nurse

Roundways will be orlright again. I bet you carn't wait to stand up and get it all sorted out, eh? I bet Mrs. Thacher'll line up something really speshul for you after that!

    You do think Nurse Roundway's hosspittal <u>should</u> have more money, don't you, Mr. Pluckley Turf?

Reguards

Andromeda Veal (Mizz)

Dear Ms Veal,

Rest assured that the issue raised in your letter of last week, is one which has received, and will continue to receive, attention commensurate with the importance attached to it by we whose responsibility it is to consider such matters in the interests of those who ultimately hold us accountable for such consideration, whoever and wherever they may or may not be. You ask me to state unequivocally my view on whether the hospital in which you are at present situated should receive an increased budget for staffing purposes, and perhaps it is your view that politicians are incapable of giving a straight answer to a question. That suggestion I must reply to by answering your question with a resounding proviso. In my own case I think I can honestly say that I have never failed to provide for those upon whom it is incumbent to take responsibility for the elicitation of appropriate responses from persons such as myself in the case of issues such as the one we are addressing, a statement of personal policy which, in terms of specific and unprejudiced concentration on aspects which by their very nature demand totally unbiased and quite unambiguous judgement, are, in a variety of nondiscriminatory ways, quite singularly oriented.

Now, to the actual circumstances pertaining to your individual environmental situation. Should the hospital in question receive extra funding for staff? I can assure you, Ms Veal, that I shall not be found guilty of that iniquitous obfuscation which invariably characterises the type of spurious response that we who humbly yet steadfastly adhere to a species of communication that cannot be described in other than superlative terms with regard to straight-forwardness and regard for what in the circumstances I am bound to refer to as the truth, have come to anticipate in a non-condemnatory but vigorously objective way, from those of our opponents who might be felt possibly to be verging on the brink of the hint of a tendency to be otherwise than open in their statements.

I hope I make myself clear.

None of us can afford, whatever our personal political and social persuasions and inclinations, to ignore the issue of staffing needs in those establishments which in time of physical and mental need carry out their statutory duties as representatives of the corporate will of the British taxpaying public in respect of necessary treatment of that aforementioned need. I reject and abhor such an attempt to side-step the responsibility for close and careful examination of such a complex and, in the atmosphere of negative and therefore potentially positive growth and prosperity prevalent at this time, purely indistinct issue as this one, which it behoves every one of us to face and explore with courage, whatever the outcome may be.

I am personally willing to exercise every ounce of energy and influence that I possess in a fully committed act of restraint with regard to unqualified acceptance of any view which does not fully comprehend the complexities of a position diametrically or obliquely opposed to such a view, and I am in total accord with those who, while decrying unconsidered allegiance to one opinion or another, are prepared to give their whole-hearted support to the proposition of retreat from acquiescence in the suggestion of any failure to act dynamically.

Need I say more? You may be sick in our hands with total confidence.

Yours faithfully,

Hugh Pluckley-Turf.

P.S. The Roundway employee whom you mention is, like all other National Health employees, entitled to days off in lieu of extra hours worked. With a little organisation she will have no further grounds for complaint. The system caters for her type of situation. Need I say more?

Dear Mister Pluckley-Turf,

Eh?

Yours facefully

Andromeda Veal (Mizz)

P.S. After reeding your bit about Nurse Roundway I looked up the end bit of your name in the dick-shunnary. It said turf is the same as another werd that starts with S and ends with D.
Need I say moor?

Dear Young Person,

(I think it best not to use your first name as I sense occult and astrological connotations in the term. Have mother and father dabbled? My anointed spouse, Stenneth and I have a special ministry in this area, not least because Stenneth, as a young person, unredeemed and adhering to the natural, was exposed to his grandfather's card trick. Thankfully, he is now released, but it is a lesson to us all.)

Your name and needs were passed to us by a friend of Anne Plass, with whom I believe you are corresponding. I am surprised that Anne failed to mention it to me herself so that Stenneth and I could offer immediate ministry. But that is so like *dear* Anne. So gloriously human, and so devoted to her husband, who is certainly *not* retarded in my view, and her son Gerald, for whom we pray constantly, that his flippancy and lack of respect will be dealt with in the fullness of time. Only last week he referred to our new assistant Elder, a tall red-haired man with a habit of blinking hard every few seconds as the 'belisha deacon'. I am sorry to report that the majority of the house group seemed to find this remark highly amusing. I prayed silently for those present, and Stenneth's outrage was such that he suffered a choking fit and was forced to leave the room. However, I do not judge Gerald. God will do that.

Now to your accident. I wonder, dear, if there is some little naughty in your life that needs to be brought under the blood. I recall an incident some months ago when Stenneth fell from the loft after climbing the ladder to procure an article for me. He had maintained that the ladder was in such a state of disrepair that it would not support his weight. I agreed therefore, to stand at the bottom of the ladder and prevent the rungs from breaking by faith. As he lay on the landing floor, moaning and clutching the base of his spine, I asked *him* if there was some little unconfessed sin in his life that was gently being pointed out to him. At that instant, before my very eyes, Stenneth was possessed by a spirit of uncontrollable anger, coming very close to a physical attack on

71

my person, shouting as he did so that the only mistake he had ever made was taking advice from 'cabbage-headed idiots who were about as spiritual as mud'. (I thought this a little hard on your Uncle Edwin, who, while not fulfilling the scriptural criteria for eldership totally, tries to do his best.) Despite Stenneth's denial, however, I was not at all surprised when, later in the day, secreted under Stenneth's portion of the nuptial mattress, I discovered an issue of a certain magazine which deals with the construction of balsa wood aeroplanes, an area wont to hold Stenneth captive in the natural, and one which he abandoned after it was revealed to me that if the number of letters in 'balsa wood' is multiplied by the age at which my saintly second cousin Maud's father died, namely 74, the resultant total is 666, the number of the 'Beast'. It

was clear to me, then, on discovering this publication, that Stenneth had been covertly feasting his eyes on illicit constructional illustrations and that his fall from the loft was a call to repentance.

So, young person, *is* there a little knot in the string of your life? If so, you must unpick it and make sure you keep your string nice and tight in future.

I have told Stenneth it is his duty to write to you, and you will be excited to hear that I may be able to visit you soon. Won't that be nice?

Yours faithfully

    Victoria Flushpool.

P.S. The Plasses do *mean* well, dear.

Dear Anne,
　　Misses Flushpool has ritten me a pecewlier letter that I don't rearly unddstand. Will you look at this coppy of the letter I have ritten back and tell me if you think it's aul right? She fritens me a bit.

　　Dear Misses Flushpool,
　　I am not shore from your letter if you are narsty or nice. Witch? I arsk myself. I don't know why you say narsty things abowt my frend Geruld. If it wosn't for his persunnel problem I wood be bawd out of my mined. Wood you lend sumone your persun-nel problem if they were horizontall in sum way? Arsk yorself that ~~wisht~~ Misses Flushpool, eh? (Have you got a persunnel problem by the way? If you havn't you ort to go down the shop and say to the man — show me yor persunnel

problems because I want one if they don't cost two much).

Annother thing – Geruld feels sorry for you, Misses Flushpool. When I staid with the Plasses I heard him say to the fashist that he thort you had a miserable old face ache. He caired about you being in payne, Misses Flushpool! And he told Anne how well ejucated you are. You must be very prowd of yor deegree in hipockrusee. Anne got mad with Geruld when he said that for sum reeson, but she smyled when he'd gone out of the room. Groan ups are a bit odd if you arsk me.

I am afrayed I didn't undastand a lot of yor letter, but you did arsk if my muther and farther had ever dabbled. I don't cwite see what it's got to do with you, Misses Flushpool, but if you must gnow, they did dabble wonce when we were on holiday in Brighten. Farther roled his trowsers up and muther helld her skert up (you coold see her nickers

75

Misses Flushpool!) and they
jumpt about on the edge of the sea.
They were cwite happy then but
when they went back the next yeer
muther met Gwenda and it aul
startid going wrong. Farther
hates Brighten now. He says you
have to be a feemale, marxist,
homersexyouall, hunchbacced dworf
with a percycution complecks if
you want to fit in at Brighten. It
must be a very funny plaice. I
thort it was just seaside.

I remember yor husband Stenneth,
Misses Flushpool. He is a smaul
man who only says Amen to that
and looks sadd when nowone's
wotching. Has he got a big
probblim of some sought? Tell
him to get Geruld to tell him
sum of his jokes. There rearly
funny, they are.

Ennyway, Misses Flushpool,
thats aul for now. Keep yor pecker
up, as farther says.

reguards

Andromeda Veal (Mizz).

P.S. Wots so wrong with my name? It's betta than being naymed after a raleway stashun like you; eh?

Well their it is, Anne. Wot do you think? She'll think a bit diffrunt abowt Geruld arfter that, eh? Perhapps she'll arsk him to tea or sumthing. I'll post it off to her twomorrow.

Logical bonds,

Andromeda.

Dear Anne,

Gosh, I was rearly suprised when Nurse Roundway came over this mourning and said you had just phoned to say doan't send that letter to Misses Flushpool. She said you sownded as if you were a bit hett up. I was just abowt to hand it in to be poasted, Anne. It's a pity rearly because I addid on a bit abowt when Geruld said that when God gave out chinns, Misses Flushpool thort he said gins and awdered a dubble. Woodn't she have larfed, Anne? Pleese let me gnow wot was wrong with sending it. I mite have cheered her up, eh?

Logical bonds

Andromeda.

(PR 19:15) (HOS 9:1) (JOHN 5:39) (ACTS 19:9)

Deep Joy Bible School;
(MAT 7:14) – Narrowpath Road – (I SAM 27:10)
Dumpton
Wessex

(JER 31:20)

Dear Andromeda,

I (GEN 6:17, EX 3:11, LEV 26:28, NUM 3:12, DEUT 7:17, JOSH 14:7, JUDG 5:3, I SAM 24:17, II SAM 3:28, JOB 1:15, EZRA 7:21, NEH 5:15, ESTH 4:16, PS 61:2, ECCL 2:25, HEB 2:13, REV 1:17, ISA 44:7, MAT 18:20) will (DEUT 21:14, JOB 13:13, PR 21:1, DAN 4:17, MAT 8:3, MARK 1:41, LUKE 5:13, MAT 20:15, MARK 14:36, JOHN 18:39, MARK 6:25, LUKE 4:6, JOHN 5:21, ACTS 18:21, ROM 7:18, I COR 4:19, PHIL 2:13, TIT 3:8, JAS 4:15, REV 11:6, DAN 4:35, COL 1:9) pray (GEN 20:7, I SAM 7:5, II SAM 7:27, EZRA 6:10, I KI 8:30, I CHR 17:25, NEH 1:6, JOB 21:15, PS 5:2, ISA 16:12, JER 7:16, ZECH 7:2, MAT 5:44, LUKE 16:27, MAT 6:5, MARK 13:18, ROM 8:26, PHIL 1:9, HEB 13:18, I TIM 2:8) for (DEUT 4:7, II SAM 11:22, PR 28:21, MAT 5:45, JOHN 1:16, ROM 13:6, II COR 5:1, II PET 3:12, MAT 6:7, II COR 13:8, MAT 25:35) you (JOSH 3:4, JOB 16:4, ISA 59:2, EZEK 11:19, AMOS 2:13, LUKE 10:16, ROM 2:24, II COR 9:4, EPH 2:1, COL 1:21, GEN 9:9, LEV 25:46, DEUT 11:4, I SAM 25:19, JER 42:16, II COR 9:14, PHIL 1:8, EX 10:16, LEV 26:17, JER 44:11, NUM 17:5, DEUT 1:44, JOSH 23:16, MI 1:2) every (GEN 6:5, LEV 19:10, NUM 5:2, I SAM 3:18, PS 119:101, PR 2:9, ISA 45:23, ROM 14:11, JER 51:29, EZEK 12:23, DAN 11:36, ZECH 12:12, MAL 1:11, MAT 4:4, MARK 1:45, LUKE 4:37, ACTS 2:43, I COR 4:17, II

COR 10:5, EPH 1:21, PHIL 2:9) **day** (GEN 1:5, EX 21:21, LEV 23:37, NUMB 3:13, DEUT 4:10, JOSH 6:10, JUDG 16:2, RUTH 4:5, I SAM 9:15, JER 15:9, NEH 4:2, ESTH 9:17, JOB 1:4, PS 19:2, PR 4:18, ISA 7:17, JER 12:3, EZEK 4:6).

Love (GEN 29:20, II SAM 1:26, PR 5:19, ECCL 9:1, JER 2:2, EZEK 16:8, DAN 1:9, HOS 3:1, MAT 24:12, JOHN 13:35, ROM 8:35, GAL 5:6, COL 1:4),

Charles

   x (PR 27:6, LUK 7:45, ROM 16:16, I THES 5:26, HOS 13:2, PS 2:12)

PART THREE

PART THREE

Dear Anne,

   Oh, Anne! Gess what, gess what! Farther John cayme to see me yesterday like he said he wood and gess what! He brort George (that's how you spel it, I do'nt gnow why), and gess what, Anne. George liked me, he did. He <u>did</u> Anne! His muther is cauled Pearl and she told Farther John it was orlright for me to meat George and he brort him and I did and he smiled at me and oh, Anne! Listan, Anne, do you gnow abowt baby's hands? Their very smaul arn't they? George's hands are very very very smaul and Farther John said lets tell eech other what we think his hands look lyke. He said he thort they were lyke littal tiney bunches of pealed prawns. That was pritty good, eh, Anne? I wanted to think of sumthing even betta, so I thort and thort about what George's littal fingas peeping out of his sleeves lookt lyke, and gess what, Anne! I rememberd when I went on the beech with Farther at Brighten and he picked up a incy littal shell from a rock pool and held it on his hand and said - Wotch this, Andy bugs! (Daddy ewsed to caul me Andy bugs, Anne). And arfter a while sum titchy littal legs cayme creeping owt of the shell and a littal creecher walked allong Daddy's hand loocking four his home in the sea. Daddy told me it was cauled a hermitt crab, Anne. They pinch shells from wincles wile their owt.

Ennyway, I said to Farther John -I think George's fingers twiddling owt of the ends of his sleeves look just lyke a littal hemitt crab's legs comming owt of his shell. And gess what, Anne. Farther John said he thort my idear was the best! Betta than the pealed prawns! Acey-pacey skill for sumone who's a horizontall attraction, eh, Anne? Farther John said he could tell George lyked me becos he loocked at me and dribbald down his nuncles brown habbit in a happee sort of way.

Then nurse Roundway came allong and said oo isan't he sweet and things and isan't he lyke his daddy (meening Father John). So I pokt her jently in the base and wissperd — he's a halibut nunc, he lives in a nunkery. Then she notissed his habit and went aul red, but Father John said it was orlright and axshully he felt flatterned. You'd think Nurse Roundway wood have more cents, woodant you, being higlee trained and aul? She's a E. S. N., you gnow. Father John says I'm George's onararary arnt. That's eggsiting, eh?

Logical bonds,

Andromeda.

P.S. Tell you sumthing, Anne. Doon't

tell ennyone else becos it sounds sillee, but when I was lying quiett jus now, do you gnow whot I thort? Father John onley rearly torks about ducks and coots and babys and things, but arfter he's gonn it feals as if Jesus has bin. Funny. eh?

Dear Geruld,
        Gottit this thyme! The persun you like is Eva Raddlemoan!

        L. B's
                Andromeda.

P.S. Eva Raddlemoan's not a little girl, is she, Geruld?

Dear Andy Pandy,

Eva Raddlemoan?! You must be joking! Another clue – this person who I like VERY MUCH has got the initials AV. Come on!!!

Love, Gerald.

Dear Child,

I am a nun in the Order of Saint Bollom of Nurd. He formed his Order in 463 and entitled it The little Brothers and Sisters of Inverted Ablution. He declined all food but squirrel droppings, and believed that God is most profoundly encountered in small purple objects immersed in badger's milk. He spent most of his life under a tree with his follower, developing the tenets by which we of the Order still live.

My name by the way is Sister Valium, and I was told of your plight by a holy Father of my acquaintance. He happened to mention the name of the hospital wherein you are constrained, and I have decided to address your soul on the qualities needful to one in your position.

First, we learn of the need for Patience from Saint Hormone of Pucket, a great intellectual of the middle ages who spent his life patiently attempting to prove his contention that the world was shaped like an aardvark's pelvis. He died in 1163 when a recalcitrant aardvark aggressively resisted his research. We revere his memory and we pray with him for that same quality of patience.

For a lesson on stillness, we turn to the work of another giant of the early church, Saint Weirdlip of Grime. Saint Weirdlip was commissioned to compose a poem on stillness by Pope Verminous the 59th in 269, and I have set the finished work down here for your edification.

> Be still, and if not still,
> Still, in not still, still be still,
> Still, until still cannot be still,
> Be still, and still be still,
> In not still. Oh, be still!

Saint Weirdlip, a great traveller, read his poem everywhere until his death in 274 when he fell off a pyramid. We remember his words and seek to attain that stillness.

Thirdly, we turn to Saint Gudgeon of Milton Keynes, a more recent teacher, to learn of the place in which we might find truth. Saint Gudgeon lived a hermit's life, preferring to remain in his Wendy House on the roof of a local fire station, emerging only to impart the newly ripened fruits of his long periods of meditation and contemplation. Saint Gudgeon delivered the following address to passers-by in a loud voice as they passed the fire station one Saturday morning.

'Brothers and Sisters, I tell you that when we seek the truth inside, it is actually outside, and when we look for it above, it is actually below, and when we hope to find it in front of us, it is actually behind us, and when we think we have found joy, we have actually found sadness, and when we are in turmoil, we are actually at peace, and when the wind blows, the air is actually very still, and when the rain falls it is actually very, very dry, and black is actually white, and get your hands off me ... !'

Unfortunately, Saint Gudgeon's address was terminated by the arrival of two uniformed persons who maintained that the peace was being disturbed, and offered him the choice of quickly returning to his Wendy House or accompanying them to the police station. Enough of his homily emerged, however, for us to learn of the search for truth, and to feel grateful for the wisdom of this holy man.

So, child, may your soul benefit from these truths and may they be an aid to swift recovery.

Benedictions,

   Sister Valium

Dear Sister Valium,

Thancyou four writing me aul that Sainte Bogwash stuff and that. My sole <u>has</u> befenittited from it. No dowt abowt that, eh? I had a Wendy house wonce becos farther bort me one, but Mother and Gwenda wood only lett me play with it if I cauled it a Willy house and put plastick Bigot inside two do the howsework, and I had to preetend to go off eech morning to do my carrear in the billding trade.

Farther got drunk once and sat innside with Bigot for hours and woodn't come owt so muther demolish-uned it aul round him and he jus sat holeding Bigot and ~~singin~~ sing-ing We shall Ovacome. That wos the end of my Willy house.

Regards to aul in the advent,

Andromeda Veal (Mizz).

Dear God,
    A frend of yors cauled Father John said it wood be aul right to write to you. As you gnow (beeing omnisheeant), I am a horizontall attraction at the moment, but I hope to be A1 lemur-wise before two long. Farther John has eggsplained to me abowt Jesus and the cross and aul. He says I can be in it if I want. I want to be in it, God, but I am afrayed you will not be getting a verry good deel.
    I was glad when muther said she cryed.   Pretty bad eh, God? Can you still have internal salvashion if yor glad yor muther cryed?   Farther John said you wood forgive ennything, but nunks do get a bit carryed away, don't they? Mined you, I do understand a bit abowt Jesus on that cross becos when Farther John said abowt it, I said it was a bit like being stretched horizon-

tall like me, only up strait. He said it was, so I said Oh, so Jesus was rearly an attraction like me? Then Father John's eyes went aul wet and he said

Yes, Andromeda, he was an attraction just like you. He smiled threw his teers, God. Does that mean there must have been a rainbow on my face? Next time Farther John came too see me, he brort me a collidoscope. It's grate God! You look threw this incy littal hole and their are all shining peaces making a ~~butful~~ butiful pattern. Farther John said I cood be a littal shining peace in the collidoscope that Jesus is, so next time you look threw a little hole at yor son Jesus yooll gnow one of the shining peaces is Andromeda Veal (Mizz).

Ennyway, the uther thing is, good luck with Muther and Farther and Gwenda. I hope you mannage to sought it aul out. Farther John says they aul got sum things wrong. It's

a big job for you, God. The larst
time I saw them aul togetha
was when Gwenda cut her finger
and farther ran and got a puncture repare outfitt. That was the
last straw. Muther told farther
to cleer off and never come back.
   Tuff one eh, God? Betta get
an ace angel on it.
      Logical bonds,
         Andromeda Veal (Mizz)

P.S. I bleeve yor acwainted with
George, who is Farther Johns neffew.
He is a sooperconfabulus baby who
likes me.   Ennyway, sumone brort
him over two the nunkery the other
day to vizit his unncle and
Father John left him with Bruther
Wilf for a minnit while he went
sumwhere. Ennyway! When he
cayme back he said that George and
Bruther Wilf (he has too tufts of
white hare sticking up from his
head, God. Do you gnow him?) were
just smiling at eech uther and
just for a ⚡ seccond he thort they

were eggsackly the sayme age!
Silly eh, God? One's verry old
and the uthers hardly borned!

P.P.S. I've adresst this to God c/o
hevven. I hop that's aul right.

Dear Geruld,
    Alan Veedordam! Eh?

        L. B's.

            Andy-pandy
    (That's what _you_
    caul me, Geruld).

Dear Andy Pandy,

Can you honestly imagine me REALLY LIKING someone called Alan Veedordam? I can't even say it. I can see I'll have to give you a lot more clues. Here goes! The person whose name is an anagram of Love and a Dream is:

(1) Someone I like VERY MUCH.
(2) Someone whose initials are AV.
(3) Someone who is in hospital with a broken leg.
(4) Someone who is eight years old.
(5) Someone who wants a bad beautiful dolly.
(6) Someone who is very pretty.
(7) Someone who I'm going to give a new personal stereo to when her birthday comes.

Love, Gerald.

Worldwide Christian Entertainment Corporation
Music for Planet Earth Project
Prefab Number 3
Armistice Row
Bagshot

Telephone (Reconnection awaits faith income)

Dear Brother or Sister,

How true it is that as one door closes another one opens. We now know and believe that the Universal Conversion College Project was meant to test our faith in preparation for the REAL task, that of organising and financing massive musical outreach events throughout the known world. Sadly, one or two of our number have left on finding that our earliest prophetic word (to the effect that the College would stand and be fruitful until the second coming) is no longer intended to be fulfilled. Regretfully, the departed brethren were unable to sustain faith in our divinely inspired change of direction, and faith, after all, is what underpins and makes possible the Lord's work.

Once again we must apologise for the even poorer quality of paper and print in our newsletter, but there are insufficient funds at present to repair our duplicating machine or to purchase new stocks of paper. Once again, however, our needs have been wonderfully met. One of our number retrieved an old John Bull child's printing set from the loft in his parents' house, and incredibly, on the very same day we discovered an anonymous gift of almost fifty sub-standard brown paper bags, simply left in the middle of the road outside our prefab. Wondrous indeed! And clear evidence that we are following the correct path.

As if more evidence was needed! It is now only weeks since it was revealed clearly that the three of us who remain are to create a powerful new musical force that will completely transform the concept of Christian music around the globe. In those weeks I have almost mastered E minor and G major on my little sister's guitar, and as funds are prayed in and it becomes possible to purchase the two missing strings, I believe in my heart that I shall be able to strum a three-chord accompaniment to 'Go Tell Aunt Rhody' by the time Christmas is here. That is not ordinary progress!

Much musical equipment will be needed, including sound systems, a range of the best guitars, drums and drum machines, keyboards of every description, special lighting effect facilities, and, of course a combination of vans and Range Rovers to transport the equipment to venues all over the world. Already we have a second-hand plectrum and a skateboard. Pledges, we believe, of the abundance that is to come. Please pray that my little sister will not notice her guitar is missing until after Christmas.

More strongly than ever we believe that we are called to live and work entirely by faith, without mentioning problems and hardships that could be alleviated by financial contributions. God knows, such difficulties abound, and, if listed, would cover several paper bags, but we are confident that the necessary funds *will* arrive and, after all, what is hunger, cold, lack of clothing and discomfort at night compared with the advancement of the Kingdom? Once more we make an impassioned plea that those who feel led to spend their money on shallow personal pleasures rather than the Lord's work should feel free to do so. We really do *not* want your cheques or postal orders (crossed and made payable to the WWCEC), unless you care.

Yours,

Vernon Rawlings (sic sec)

P.S. News of musical venues will follow. Eventually we hope to perform at Las Vegas, Wembley Arena, the Shea Stadium, and in Red Square. Our only actual booking at present is Stanley (my assistant) playing the spoons at amateur night in the public bar of the Frog and Spittle just down the road from the prefab. We really are looking for a miracle here, as we possess only one spoon and Stanley has never done it before.

Dear Geruld,
        Oh, Geruld! It was me!
Oh, Geruld. Love and a dream.
Oh, Geruld!

        L. B's.

        Andromeda Veal.
        (Andy-pandy) X.

Dear Farther John,

How are you and aul the uther halibuts? How is Bruther Wilf? I have dun a pichure of him to hang on his sell door. I bet heel be the onley one in the nunkery to have an eriginal Veal. One day in the fucher they'll sell it at Smotherbee's action rooms for trillyons and trillyons of pownds, and Brother Wilf's grate granchildrun will be as rich as acey-pacey Cliff Richud. Oh no! I forgott nunks doon't have baybies, do they? Well he cood leave it too the nunkery if he wants, so they can train up new Bruther Wilfs in the fucher. I hope he lykes my pichure. I did it four him becos he did yor work for you while you torked to God abowt coots and that, down by the lapping lake.

Listan, Farther John! Gess

what's happerned! I doon't gnow
if I menshunned it too you, but
I have nevver had a dolly
eggsept plastick Bigot and he
was a vicktim of dumbestic
vilence.   Gwenda said that in
the new aje arfter the reverlooshun wimmin woodn't be miss-
lead by such divices. She said
wimmen get a ror deal aul
round becos men ewes them. She
said sheed never   aggree to
show her nakid body on page
threee of the tablet press, then
farther said he'd lyke to prerpose
a vote of thanks on beeharf
of aul men evvrywhere, and it
aul got a bit vilent again.
Ennyway, Muther said I
wosn't to have a dolly becos
dollys are bad and I said I
doon't wont one ennyway if
their bad. But, Father John, I
wosn't telling the trooth! Ooh
Father John, I did wont a dolly
so much! Ennyway! In a letta
to my frend Geruld (he's going

to give me my verry own ~~xxxx~~
persunnel problem soon by the way)
I sought of hinted that I
woodn't mind having a dolly,
eeven though they are bad
things. Gess what! He sumhow
got the hint! I slept aul
threw viziting this morning
and when I woke up - gess what!
Their was anuther head on the pillo
necst to mine. It was a big
dolly! A dolly, Farther John!
She is luvvly and pritty and in
a bewtiful dress and their
was a note pinnd to her dress
and what do you think it said?
Are you shaking yor hed in the
nunkery and saying — no, I
doon't gnow what it said?
Are you, Farther John? I'll
tell you. It said,
    MY NAME IS LUCKY LUCY.
Then on the uther side it said
— We have called her Lucky Lucy
because we think she's very, very
lucky to belong to such a nice
little girl, from Anne, Geruld.

and the fashist.

Oh, Father John, I cuddal my Lucky Lucy aul the thyme, but cood you say to God that duzn't meen he can slip off too the lapping lake too do a bitt of coot' bilding. I wont to show my Lucky Lucy to muther and farther soon.

Logical bonds to you
and Brother Wilf

Andromeda

P.S. Did you gnow that I am a nammagranamm of Love and a dream? Geruld said. Good, eh?

P.P. S. Cood you drop me a note eggsplaining the trinnity?

Dear Anne, Geruld and nice fashist,
 I found my dolly that you brort.
 I lyke her name.
 She is grate.
 How do you say thancyoo when you won't it to sound big?
 Thancyoo
 THANCYOO

Logical Bonds,

Andy-pandy and Lucky Lucy.

P.S. Their mite be sum kissis cumming yor way when I'm verticall again.

Hi, Andy Pandy!

Glad you liked Lucky Lucy. She's a real doll, and so are you! I see the fashist has become a *good* fashist. You should've seen Dad's face when he read that. He's an old softy really. We all went to choose your dolly together, and you've never heard anything like Dad. Fussy? It was amazing! Clothes the wrong colour, ears the wrong shape, hair too long, hair too short, nothing was right. In the end he disappeared down behind this long counter to look at some dolls in boxes on the shelves. Just after he'd dropped out of sight, the lady who manages the shop came up and said to me, 'Is there something I can help you with now, sir?'

Before I could say anything, Dad's voice seemed to answer her from behind the counter.

'No! You're not pretty enough, and your knickers are falling apart!'

You know I don't get easily embarrassed, Andy Pandy, but I could feel myself going red.

'He doesn't mean you,' I said, 'he means ...'

'As for your so-called body, it's hardly human, let alone female! Back in your box, yer ratbag!'

I explained that Dad was talking to the dolls under the counter, but that just made her very nervous instead of annoyed. Dad was mortified when he realised what had happened, so we got out quick after that and found Lucky Lucy in another shop. Your Nurse Roundway let us put her next to you while you were asleep.

Anyway! I ran into Father John yesterday on his way to speak at some meeting, and he told me you'd asked him to 'drop you a note eggsplaning the Trinity'. Good one, Andy Pandy! He was going to write back to you, but I said hold on a minute, because last Sunday we had a talk in church on the meaning of the Trinity, and I was pretty sure Dad would have got it all down in his blessed diary, especially as the 'talk' turned out to be – well, you'll see what I mean! Dad says you're very welcome to see this bit. Hope you enjoy it. I think it's *wonderful!*

Saturday

Leonard Thynn round tonight. Says he's volunteered to explain the Trinity at church tomorrow. Bit surprised really. He can hardly find his way home, let alone clarify one of the greatest theological mysteries of all. Gerald said he was looking forward to it, and did we know that theology is an anagram of 'O, get holy!'?

Sunday

Church.

Thynn started by dragging a horrible rusty old electric fire out to the front. Plugged it into a socket at the side, then faced the congregation looking rather pleased with himself.

He said, 'Right! Trinity! Easily explained. When I switch on at the mains in a moment, I want all of you, but 'specially the children, to watch very, very closely, and see if you can spot what happens. Ready? Here we go! Keep those eyes skinned, or you might miss it!'

Suddenly felt glad I was sitting at the back. When Thynn pushed the switch down there was a loud bang and a shower of sparks. Leonard screamed and stumbled back into Doreen Cook's lap. Several children put their hands up.

Little Dotty Rawlings called out, 'I saw, I saw! It blowed up and frightened you! Is that what the Trinity means Mr Thynn?'

Leonard got up and faced us again. Looked rather white and his hair was sticking up on end. He said, 'Sorry about that, everybody. Little light should have come on, and I was going to say that was like Jesus, and then I was going to say that the electricity was like the Holy Spirit, and then ... well, never mind. Hang on ... !

Dashed over to the side and came back with an ancient old hoover. Switched the mains switch off, unplugged the electric fire, and plugged in the hoover. Dotty Rawlings leaned forward excitedly. Everyone else ducked.

Leonard said, 'Right! Another idea of mine – really explains the Trinity. Ready, children? When I switch on, watch what it does. Better put your fingers in your ears. Makes a bit of a racket. Here goes!'

Entire congregation flinched as Thynn switched on. Nothing at all happened. Children's hands went up again.

'It doesn't work!' squeaked Dotty Rawlings. 'The Trinity doesn't work, does it, Mr Thynn?'

Leonard turned the hoover upside down and stared sadly at it. He said, 'Hmm ... I *was* going to say that it sweeps as it beats as it cleans, and that's a bit like the old Trini – '

Mrs Flushpool rose like an iceberg to interrupt, 'That is the mediaeval heresy of modalism, Mr Thynn!'

'No,' said Thynn, poking absently at the machinery with his finger, 'I think it's just a coin stuck in the whatsit.'

Leonard ran out of appliances at this point so we went on to the choruses ...

Monday

Thynn round for coffee tonight, also Frank Braddock, our neighbour. Told Frank about yesterday and asked him how *he* would explain the Trinity.

He lit his pipe and said, 'You know, there are four things I like about the Trinity. First, I love having a father in God. Second, I love having a friend and brother in Jesus. Third, I love having a comforter and guide in the Holy Spirit. And fourth ...'

Anne and I said, 'Yes?'

'Fourth, I love the fact that it's a mystery. God in three persons. Three persons – one God. It's a mystery and I love it. Why would I want to spoil things by trying to explain it?'

'Mmmm ...' muttered Thynn, who wasn't listening, 'maybe if I'd used an automatic toaster ...'

Great, eh, Andy Pandy? Isn't Leonard wonderful! See you soon – love to Lucky Lucy.

Gerald.

Pope John Pall,
The Fattycan,
Roam,
Italy.

Dear Pope,
	Aul right so I'm knot a roaming catlick, but befor you rush off to give an ordinance to sumone in annother part of the Fattycan just considder this. I have got a frend called Farther John who is as big a halibut as you are and I bet he gets interupptid by God near gooses and coots just as mutch as you do. (My name is Mizz Andromeda Veal by the way. I am horizontall till the lemur recuvvers).
	Our cherch is not cwite like yors, Pope. We do not have trainsinsubstandardstations at our commyunion, we aul come in cars, but we do have the same things to eat and drink as yor lot, only littal mingy bits tho, and letts face it Pope, the persunn in charje

of our cherch duzzn't faul
flat on his face evvery time he
steps off an airyplane like you
do. Carn't we aul joyne together,
Pope. We cood ion out our
diffrunces. For instans, you say
babies have got to be abul to do
the limbo to get into hevven.
Isn't that a bit unfare, Pope?
Why shood littal babies have to
limbo unda the gaites. Their
too smaul to lern, I reckon. I
can't do it very well and I'm
eight! Lett's leave that won out
eh, Pope? Get all your cardigan-
s together and do a bull on
them abowt it. I'm shore aul
the uther roaming catlicks will
aggree with you. In retern we
coold say you doan't have to
climb the thirty nine steps to
wear an angular preest's hood.
Fare? I think so. By the way,
isn't their one of your monseenyers
who goes on abowt crude rissoles
like the green and common
wimmen. He mite gnow my muther

and her frend Gwenda. I havn't
seen my muther since I started
being an attraction but Father
John has had a werd with God
about it and its aul in hand.
He's a nunk you see Pope.
        Hears to yunitty!

        Andromeda Veal (Mizz)

P.S. I hear you are a bitt of a
poet, Pope. Well, hears a coinside-
nse – so am I!!! I have writed a
poem speshully for you.

    I'm not a roaming catlick,
    And I sinseerly hope,
    That lodes of preying cardigans,
    Will never make me Pope.

    I doan't think I'm a anglian,
    I'd hayte to wear a hassock,
    Or be like Rabbit Runcie,
    And gneel apon a cassock.

    I gnow who startid metherdists,
    John Wesslee did of corse,

But I'm no good at showting,
And I cannott ryde a hoarse.

I doont think I'm a batpist,
I even hayte the rain!
When they poosh me in the warter,
Will I come upp againe?

I cood go to a howse church,
But I am rather bad,
At looking verry happy,
When I am fealing sad.

Why doon't we start a nue ~~chur~~
            cherch, Pope,
Where evvrything is reel?
I've eeven got a nayme for it—
The cherch of John Pall Veal.

            Aperson.

PART FOUR

PART FOUR

Dear Andromeda,

My name is Frank Braddock. I live next door to Adrian and Anne Plass who I know are good friends of yours. Another person we are both friendly with is Father John. Years and years ago, we were at school together, although in those days we called each other by nicknames. His was Bungles, and mine was Smelly! You'll never guess why I was called Smelly, and I'm sure as eggs not going to tell you. The only smelly thing about me now (I hope!) is my pipe. I've found some delicious black-cherry scented tobacco, and I must admit it is rather powerful stuff. I don't think they'd want it stinking out the wards at this hospital you've landed yourself in.

Now, the reason I've written is to pay back a favour. You don't even realise you've done me a favour, do you? Well you have, and I'll tell you what it was. When you came to stay with the Plasses some months ago, you went to church with them and, although I go somewhere else usually, I just happened to be at their church on that particular Sunday. Your Uncle Edwin invited me along I think. Halfway through the service you stood up on your chair when the organist struck up, and sang 'SHE IS LORD ...' at the top of your voice. Then the organist fellow panicked and went into 'Home, home on the range', and all was chaos. Well, ever since then, whenever I've felt a little low, I think of that day, and the organist's face, and one or two folk with their arms in the air singing '... where the deer and the antelope play ...', and I just can't stop a little chuckle from tickling its way up from inside me somewhere and forcing its way out through a smile. So thank you very much for giving me a way to cheer myself up, and that's what I'm paying you back for.

Right! So what am *I* giving *you?* Not much I'm afraid. I'm going to tell you a story. That's my job you see – trying to write things that other people might want to read. I asked Bungles – I mean Father John – if he thought it was a good idea, and he said yes, he thought you would be good at reading stories. (He asked

117

me, by the way, to say that the halibut nunk sends all his logical bonds). Now, here's the story. Hope you enjoy it!

Once upon a time, in a world almost exactly like ours, but with an extra thimbleful of opportunity for strange and exciting things to happen, there lived a little girl in a tall brown house. Now, I know there is nothing wrong with the colour brown. Chocolate ice-cream is dark, tasty brown, Hair can be a lovely shining brown. Some people have warm brown skins. Conkers, chestnuts, horses, birds, new shoes and little girls' eyes can all be brown and beautiful. I know that. But the house that this little girl lived in was a quite different kind of brown. It was a dead, hopeless, given-up sort of brown, an embarrassed, dingy, never-was-smart brown, and it was everywhere. I expect, when I say it was everywhere, you don't really think I mean it, do you? You think that there must have been a few yellows, a patch of red here and there, one or two orange things perhaps, some pictures on the wall with bright colours shining against the dull brownness, and, of course, whole expanses of blue sky and maybe green grass to be seen through the windows, not to mention the faces of all the people who lived in the tall brown house. Their faces can't have been that horrible brown colour, you're thinking. I tell you it was *everywhere!*

Walls, ceilings and floors – brown. Pictures, ornaments, furniture, curtains, lampshades, light bulbs, carpets, books, cups, saucers, plates, bowls, knives, forks – all brown. There might very possibly have been eggshell blue skies, and emerald lawns on the other side of the windows, but it was impossible to tell because every pane of glass was heavily tinted in one overwhelming colour – brown. There was a bird in a brown cage. He was a parrot. He ran up and down his brown ladder, looked at his brown face in his brown shaded mirror, pecked brown seed from the brown sandpaper on the floor of his cage, and had learned to say only one thing – 'Brown Polly! Brown Polly! Brown Polly!' Even the water that ran from the brown taps was brownish. It was used to make brown squash and brown tea, and brown coffee and brown Andrew's liver salts. Please believe me when I say that *everything* was brown. Brown, brown, brown, brown, brown! It was all – brown!

Now here's an embarrassing thing. I've just remembered that one thing wasn't brown. It was a book. It was the little girl's most secret and most precious thing, and she hid it very, very, very carefully in a brown space underneath the brown wardrobe where her brown clothes hung. She'd found it one day right at the back of the big bookcase in the sitting room, and when she opened it, it was as though someone had suddenly punched a book-sized hole through one of the brown-tinted windows. The colours seemed to fly up and dance around in front of her face like music that you could see. She felt quite light-headed and dizzy after only a few seconds, and had to shut the book quickly for fear of falling down. She didn't tell her mother and father about her find. She guessed somehow that they would take it away from her if they knew. So she carried it quickly up to her room and pushed it beneath the wardrobe. Every day since then, when the coast was clear, she had knelt down on her bedroom carpet, slid her hand into the secret space, and, with a little fluttery tickling feeling in her tummy, drawn out the book and feasted her eyes on the bright pages. For a long time that was enough. Just to know that brown was not all was a thrilling secret, but as the weeks went by, and the little girl grew older, she knew that she would have to sit her Mother and Father down one day and ask them to explain their brown attitudes.

The day came. Mother and Father were sitting in their brown armchairs in the brown sitting-room drinking brown drinks from brown glasses. Father was wearing a brown suit. Mother was wearing an old brown artist's smock over a pair of brown jeans. The little girl, whose name was Tanya, came into the room holding something behind her back.

'Mother and Father,' she said, 'I have a question to ask you.'

Father looked at her brownly. He had a thick brown moustache, long brown sideboards, and thin brown straggly hair. When he wasn't completely happy he rubbed at the side of his nose with his thumb. He was doing it now.

'Ask your question, Tanya,' he said. 'I will try to answer it.'

'Why is everything brown?' said Tanya, quietly and seriously.

Father laughed a clockwork laugh.

'That is not a real question,' he said. 'That is like saying, "Why has everyone got two legs?" Everything is brown because everything is brown. That is the way it is – brown.'

'Is there only brown?' whispered Tanya.

'Yes,' said Father stiffly.

Mother looked worried.

'Why am I not allowed to see through the door when you open it? Why don't we ever open the windows? When am I going to go outside? Why have you told me fibs? Look!'

Tanya swung the open book from behind her back and held it out (open at the most colourful page) towards Mother and Father. Mother gave a little scream and put her hand over her mouth. Father stood up as though a spring had exploded in the armchair and shot him to his feet.

'WHERE DID YOU GET THAT?' he shouted.

'It's mine,' said Mother in a small wavery voice, 'I had it when I was a little girl.'

'I found it,' said Tanya. 'It's not brown. Why didn't you tell me the truth?'

'We thought it best,' said Mother tearfully. 'Colours can be dangerous.'

'Brown is safe,' said Father. 'It is our sort of colour. We did it for you. Why should you be confused by reds and blues and greens and golds and yellows and purples? We had big, big problems, all because of colours. We want you to stay in a brown world and not worry. Outside is a colour jungle. Stay in and tell yourself that all you need is brown.'

'No!' said Tanya, 'I am allowed to be confused too! I *want* to go in the jungle! I *hate* brown! Open that big window!'

She pointed towards the big brown-tinted French windows. All her life they had been closed. Outside, brown flowers bloomed sadly beside brown grass under brown trees as they had always done.

'If you don't open that window *now*,' said Tanya firmly. 'I shall shut my eyes and never, never open them again!'

Mother and Father looked at each other.

Father rubbed his nose *very* hard with his thumb.

120

'Shall I?' he said.

'Yes,' said Mother.

Father walked over and forced the rusty old brown bolts back. He pushed the windows open. The room was flooded with light and colour. As Father stepped back Tanya ran to the open space and gazed with bright excited eyes at this dazzling world she had never seen. Looking back, she saw that Mother and Father were standing side by side, holding hands. They seemed a little bit older, and a little bit smaller, but, to her surprise, they looked a lot less brown and, for the first time for a long time, they were smiling.

God be with you, Andromeda.

Love, Frank Braddock.

Dear Cliff Richard,
          Orlright so I'm onely eight
and I carn't play tennis and I
havun't got a exy flash nayme like
Nivea Looting John, and I havun't
maid records like her abowt drinking lemmonaid wen its hot cauled
Let's get fizzy cool and I carn't do
mutch at the moment ennyway becos
I'm an ongoing attraction in hospi-
tall until the lemur getts its akt
togetha, and muther is still up with
Gwenda and the green and common
wimmen and aul, but why shoodun't
we get marrid when I am bigger?
Arfter aul, you doon't seem to get
enny older.   One thing tho, yew'll
have to be a bit more soshulist
with yor cash or Gwenda will
nevver let muther let us get
ingaged. And let's face it, yor
pritty near a trillionair, eh? You
cood have as menny personnul
problems as you lyke with no cwestions arsked. It's orlright for sum!

My frend Geruld (doon't tell him
I've writed to you, will you Cliff?
He's seccond choise and he mite get
a bit annoyde. Gnow what I mean?)
has onley got one persunnel probbli-
m , and thats on lone to me as
long as I'm horizontall. I bet
you've gived one to Mank Harvin and
all the uther shaddoes and still
got munny over. I bet you have,
Cliff!

Lissan! Annother thing we've got
going four us, Cliff- we're both
beleevers, so it won't be a mixt mar-
rije, and you can arsk yor frend
Billee Greyham to marree us, becos
he is an ordrained batpist as long as
he isn't bizzy getting peeple up owt
of there seats at the thyme. This
necks bit took aul of yesterday to
work out, Cliff. I was abul to do it
becos of muther havving aul yor old
reccords at home. Eeven Gwenda
said that wen she was a young
gullabul girl she lyked you. She
said — he ewsed to make my legs go
all funnee — and farther said – O

, that's wot did it is it? – and
muther tipt his bubbul and squeek
down the waste dissposul.
   Ennyway! Hear it is. See if yew can
spot yor old reccords, Cliff.

   If yew wont to go on beeing
   one of THE YOUNG ONES yewd
   betta marry this LIVING
      DOLL cauled Andromeda and
      stop beeing a BACHELOR BOY,
    then arfterwoods we'll go
      TRAVELLING LIGHT on our
      SUMMER HOLIDAY and if
      ennything getts in our way
   we'll MOVE IT.
      Sighed,
         Yor DEVIL WOMAN
            Andromeda ♡

Acey-pacey skill, eh Cliffy baiby? Did
you spott the songs?
   Ennyway! Nurse Roundway's cumming to put powder on my base in a
minnit. Horizontall = sore, Cliff!
Say hallow to the shaddoes four me,
      Logical Bonds

Andromeda Veal (Mizz)

P.S. Wen you were smaul, were you black with curlly hair and did you scream songs that sownded lyke Bee droppt a loofah she's my baibee or sumthin?

Dear Andromeda,

I hope you don't mind me writing you a little note. I am Lucky Wilf. I am just as lucky as the beautiful dolly that Father John has told me about, because I now have a wonderful picture on the wall of my room. A present from a little girl. Nothing could be more precious. I don't deserve to have it, but I *do* thank you for drawing it specially for me. I am very old, and not very good, but I do know that every now and then God decides that old Wilf needs a little something. *You* helped him this time. Thank you, Andromeda, so much.

Love in the name of my Master,

Brother Wilf.

Dear Bruther Wilf,

I'm pleesed you think my pichure is acey-pacey skill. Lissan! I writed a poem four the Pope the uther day, but now I want to wright one abowt baiby George for Farther John whoo's his uncel as I eggspect you gnow. I hope you ~~doh~~ do'ont mined, but I'm sending it to you to see if it's good enuff. If it's exy acey-pacey grate you can tell me it is, butt if you thinc it's pritty crabby stuff can you preetend it's not two bad but not cwite good enuff? Eh? Thancs, Bruther Wilf. Hear's the poem.

God maid George.
by
Andromeda Veal (Mizz)
Age 8

God maid George
A fat littal packit of foot on the end of eech leg,

God maid George
A smile aul cleen and speshul
   from his tummy
God maid George
Wispee moheecan hair, he's a tuffee
      God maid George
His fisty waives say I'm alive, I am!
                              I am!

   God maid George
No narsty bits or nauty bits he's
   onley just unpakked.
   God maid George
And he told George to smile at me, I
   nearly cryed, I did,
God maid George
      Sumtimes Georges cum owt
wrong, there braynes and boddies
            aren't maid right
   God maid them two
God luvs aul the Georges.

Does he luv them aul Bruther Wilf?
Not justhe aulright ones, eh?
            Logical Bonds
               Andromeda Xx

P.S. How old ar yew, for goodniss

sake?

P. P. S.   I hope the kissis ar aulright four a halibut.

My dear Andromeda,

You make me feel so humble. Fancy asking *me* if I think your beautiful poem is good enough to present to Father John! I have not had the pleasure and privilege of meeting little George, but after reading your poem I could almost see him sitting in front of me, smiling and waving his fists to show me he is 'alive – he is! he is!'. As for the 'fat littal packit of foot on the end of each leg', oh, Andromeda, I think that is a marvellous description. I really don't know how you think of these things. Of *course* you must give the poem to Father John. His eyes will light up. They do that you know, when something special happens. I know – I've seen them.

Andromeda, may I ask you a big favour? As you will see I have sent the piece of paper that the poem is written on back to you with this letter. I wonder if you would be kind enough to give me permission to copy it out when you have sent it to Father John? I would like to put it on my wall beside my picture. That would be a real joy! Do say it's alright.

You are quite right of course when you say that some Georges – some babies – are not made right, and you asked me if God loves them just as much. Well, I'm sure he does, but, Andromeda, I must be honest with you. When I was a young monk I used to get very angry indeed with God. 'Why,' I used to say, 'when you are supposed to be able to do anything, and you are supposed to love everybody, do you let little babies be born with things wrong with them? Why, God? Tell me!' Oh, I *did* get ratty, Andromeda, and I didn't seem to get any answers at all. So I went along to someone called Brother Arnold (he was about as old then as I am now, and much, much wiser) and told him all about it. He listened and smiled and didn't say anything for a long time, then he said, 'Wilf, I want you to go and kneel in the little chapel and look at the cross on the altar, and as you kneel there I want you to say these words over and over again quite quietly to yourself – "He's in it with us – he's in it with us," then come back and tell me what you think. I'll be waiting here.'

We had a wonderful little private prayer chapel at that place, Andromeda. It was very small, not much bigger than a fairly big pantry, and there was just enough room for one person to kneel at a sort of desk thing in front of the altar. On the altar there was only a white cloth and a silver crucifix, and you had to take a candle in a brass holder from a little shelf at the side, light it with a match from the box that was always kept there, and stand it on the altar just in front and to the side of the crucifix, so that the cross was lit up by a gentle yellow glow.

That's what I did that day. Then I knelt at the desk and looked at the crucifix in front of me.

You know what a crucifix is, don't you, Andromeda? It's a cross with the figure of Jesus hanging on it. Some people don't like them. They say that Jesus rose from the dead and he's alive, so the cross should be empty. I know what they mean, and actually the big cross in the main chapel at both places where I've lived *is* an empty one, but I always thought it was right for Jesus to be there on the cross in that tiny little private chapel. I'll tell you why. You see, every day, however hard I try, I end up doing the sort of things that Jesus took the blame for on the cross. We all do. That's why he did it. He knew we'd never be good enough on our own. And every day God forgives me very enthusiastically. He says, 'Don't be discouraged, Wilf! Start again, old chap,' and I do. So you see – in a way – I put Jesus back on that horrible cross every day, and every day he dies, is buried, and rises again in me when I'm forgiven. That's why it's good to be reminded of what he did when I'm alone in the little chapel. The crucifix does that.

So, I knelt there for a while, as Brother Arnold had said I should, and repeated those words quietly and slowly, over and over again.

'He's in it with us, He's in it with us, He's in it with us …'

Jesus' face had been very well made by whoever modelled that crucifix. There was an expression of such pain and sweetness in his eyes, and he seemed to be looking straight at me, like those photos where the eyes follow you wherever you go in the room.

And when I stopped saying those words, it was as if *he* started to speak.

'I'm in it with you, I'm in it with you, I'm in it with you ...'

And then, Andromeda, I just started to cry. It sounds silly doesn't it, but I couldn't stop myself. The funny thing was, though, they weren't really *my* tears – they were *his*. He was showing me how *he* felt.

I went back to Brother Arnold a little later and he said, 'Well?'

I just nodded. I couldn't think what to say, and I didn't actually have any more answers than I'd had before, but I did understand that God cares for and grieves over 'the Georges that come out wrong' much much *much* more than I ever could. Beyond that it's just a mystery, Andromeda.

Try to trust Him. He adores *you!*

Love and thanks,

Brother Wilf.

Dear Andromeda,

Thynn here again – Leonard Thynn. Friend of the Plasses, remember? Sent you that hilarious – well, quite hilarious – joke about the smallish squatter behind the thingy – tree. Gottit? Good. Well, thought I'd write again with another joke – well, more an anecdote than a joke, although it's meant to *be* funny – sort of a story with a funny bit at the end, if you know what I mean.

Anyway – this joke, anecdote, or story with a funny bit at the end – tell you what – let's call it an anecdotal story with a funny bit at the end from now on just to simplify matters. Okay? Right! Where was I? Oh, yes ... this anecdotal story with a funny bit at the end starts – well, obviously it starts, doesn't it? I mean, in a sense, as soon as you say you're going to tell it, it's already started, hasn't it, although technically it could be said to have – sorry, wittering on again. Bad habit. No problem at all after a few drinks – not that that's a good reason to drink, young Veal! Good heavens, no! Just happens to be a fact that – what was I saying? Oh, yes, of course! This anecdotal story with a funny bit at the end starts in a prison. Well, I say a prison, but I suppose it could be a detention centre, or a borstal, or (depending on the old historical perspective) a prisoner-of-war camp, or even a jolly old police cell – not that there's anything very jolly about police cells. Been in a couple I'm afraid, after getting err ... getting err ... arrested, as it were. No, not very jolly, but err ... the chap in this anecdotal story with a funny bit at the end happens to be locked up in a prison, detention centre, borstal, prisoner-of-war camp or police cell, and one day he says to himself – probably not out loud – well, maybe out loud if he's been in there a long time – he says, 'I want to get out.' Sounds from that as though he's English, but actually the chap could be any nationality at all. Could be Chinese or Ukrainian or Slav or Patagonian or Scottish – mind you if he was Scottish he'd probably speak in English anyway, unless he was fanatically devoted to the re-establishment of the Gaelic language in which case he'd presumably – mind you, even if he was Chinese he might have been brought up in – say, Luton, in which case he'd probably speak English with a Chinese accent, one would guess.

Anyway, this chap in the prison, borstal, detention centre, prisoner-of-war camp or police cell, says to himself in his own particular language, accent, dialect, or patois, 'I want to get out.' And then – to cut a long story short – well, significantly shorter anyway – he says it again, and this time he really means it. Not that he didn't mean it the first time. It's just that the second time he err ... meant it more. More than the first time, that is.

So, the chap (of uncertain nationality) digs a hole in the floor of his cell – if that's what he's in. Well, he must be in *some* sort of cell, unless he's a member of staff, in which case he wouldn't need to dig a ... where was I? Ah, right! He digs a hole. Don't know how he does it. Not a practical chap myself. Once got Radio Four on the hoover when I was trying to fix the iron. Bit of a surprise really. Good programme though – all about the Watusi Tribe of Central Africa. Amazing people! Apparently they never, never – sorry, mustn't get side-tracked – spoils the err ... anecdotal story with a funny bit at the end. He digs a hole, so that he can burrow out – tunnel out's better. 'Burrow' sounds a bit too rabbit-like really, don't you think? – he tunnels through the ground and comes out in the street outside. More good luck than good management, I'd say, unless he had special knowledge of the prison – which he might have done. Let's be fair! You don't get told that when you hear the joke – not that it matters – much ...

Yes, well, anyway – he climbs out of the thingy – the hole, and he shouts out (in English or Chinese or Ukrainian or Slav or English with a Scottish accent, or Gaelic, or English with a Chinese/Luton accent) 'I'm free! I'm free!'

And then (the funny bit at the end of the anecdotal story is virtually imminent here, Andromeda), a little boy who happens to be passing – and, unless the digging chap has managed to burrow (tunnel rather) right through to another continent, he's presumably the same nationality as the digging chap – says (and this is the actual funny bit at the end of the anecdotal story) 'That's nothing – I'm four!'

Get it? 'I'm free! I'm free!' 'That's nothing – I'm four'. What a scream, eh? Well, anyway ...

All the best, young Veal. Don't fret now. Got the boss on our side. Know what I mean? Mother sends her love by the way. Says if she can put up with me for thirty-mumble years, you'll survive your hospital experience.

Regards,

Leonard (Thynn)

P.S. When you're better, you must (well, if you want to – no 'must' about it) come round and see what I've taught the Plasses' cat to do. You'll be amazed – well, very surprised anyway ...

Dear Andromeda,

It was with abundant joy that I received the wonderful news of your hospitalisation. How marvellous to suffer as you are doing! What a depth of gratitude and deep thankfulness you must be experiencing as you lie in the privileged position of one who is allowed to enjoy pain and discomfort hour after hour and day after day.

Hallelujah!

How you must delight in and chuckle over those verses which reveal the inestimable benefits of regular immersion in the rich baptism of physical anguish. How I envy you your glorious opportunity to participate in the ecstasy of awful agony. Oh, to break a femur! What happiness! To slip and crash to the ground causing serious injury necessitating a long period of intensive institutional care! What could be more welcome? How your faith must be blossoming in the invigorating atmosphere of profound disability that surrounds you now! With what deep happiness I am sure you must survey those heavy weights depending from your helpless limbs, and look forward with a mighty leaping of your spirit to a further lengthy experience of enforced horizontality! On Saturday I shall be enabled to witness your good fortune personally when I am home for a weekend from college. I shall enter your ward with a dance of elation and greet you with a word of celebration.

Yours in joyful anticipation,

Charles Cook.

Dear Geruld,

You gnow your friend
Charles at Deep Joy Bibul school
who sends me pecewliar letters?
Well the last one was all abowt
how fracchering your lemur and
being an attraction was acey-
pacey   brilliant and all.
Loony, eh?

Ennyway, he came to see me
on saterday and he dansed into
the ward not loocking where he
was going and   stubbed his
big   toe on the end of a big
mettal thing and startid hopp-
ping dround saying bad words
threw his teeth. It was grate!
I decided to cheer him up
Geruld, so I said — Oh to stub
a toe! What happinness! What
ridundant joy to have a acey-pacey
pain in the foot! I wish I
was lucky old you hopping
abowt, Charles old chap! Let's
hope the luvvly agony larsts a

137

good long time, eh? Hallylooyah!
    He was very cross for a
littal while, Geruld, then he
suddernly laughed, and he was
nice like he ewesed to be and
not like a robot. They must have
speshul robot classes down at
his school, eh? Do you have to
get speshul permishun to be
normal when yor a christiun,
Geruld? If you don't, somewon
ought to tell evvryone. I think
so.
        All my Logical Bonds

            Andromeda.

Dear Andromeda,

I met Father John in the off-licence the other evening, and we were chatting about you. He said how much he'd enjoyed getting to know you, and how bravely he thought you were putting up with being stuck in that hospital bed and not having Mum and Dad around. One or two of the things he said made me think that you might be feeling a bit useless to God, and even worrying that you weren't good enough for him. When I talked to Anne about this she said I ought to send you the bit from my 'diary' when I had to give a talk on Spiritual Pride. She said, 'If God's still crazy about you despite things like that, then there's hope for anybody.' A bit of an exaggeration in my view, but it is true that I was rather thoughtless, and I'm sure you wouldn't have made the same mistakes. Father John says we're all members of the ratbag club, so we'd better stick together all we can, eh?

Anyway, here's my 'diary'. Your friend Leonard Thynn is in most of it ...

Wednesday

Very flattered by Edwin asking me to speak on the subject of Spiritual Pride at next Sunday's service. Don't know why, but whenever I'm asked to do something like this, my spirituality seems to be cubed on the spot. Came away from the phone wanting to tell someone (in a humble sort of way) about Edwin's invitation. There was only Thynn there. He'd come round earlier for a meal without being invited *again*. I said, 'Edwin wants me to speak on Spiritual Pride next Sunday. I can't think why.'

'Because you're an expert on it I expect,' said Thynn, leaning back and taking the last pear from the fruit bowl.

Didn't bother to ask him what he meant. Why did God create things like locusts and earthquakes and Thynn?

I'm determined to do this talk really well. Must think of three headings beginning with the same letter ...

Thursday

Thynn round tonight. Why doesn't he just move in and have done with it? Invited himself to go with Gerald to a meeting at some new local church. Asked which church it was. Gerald said it called itself the Holy and Apostolic True Church of the Abundant Revelation of Living Stones. Apparently it's a split from a breakaway group which left the remnant of a disaffected portion of a dissenting faction from a fellowship that had separated itself from the original Holy and Apostolic True Church of the Abundant Revelation of Living Stones. According to Gerald, none of the present members realise that they've dissented themselves right back to the place where they started. I sometimes wonder if Gerald makes these things up ...

Settled down after they'd gone out to plan my talk. Used a new concordance so that I can whizz from scriptural reference to scriptural reference like a real speaker. Managed to sort out two of my headings as 'Humility' and 'Holiness'. Bit stuck for a third, but it'll come!

Friday .

Very difficult to work on my talk this evening. Thynn arrived at teatime and stayed until late. He and Gerald get very silly sometimes. Tonight they played Cluedo, substituting the names of church members for the traditional ones. In the first game it turned out that Mrs Flushpool did it in the study with the candlestick; in the second one Richard Cook did it with a rope in the kitchen. Found all the cackling very off-putting. Eventually they noticed my tutting and asked what I was doing. Made the mistake of telling them I was searching for a third heading beginning with 'H'. I must be mad. They suggested Henry Cooper, Haggis, Horstead Keynes, Halitosis, Hippopotamus, Heatrash, Ham rolls, and many, many more. Gerald doesn't seem to appreciate that this Spiritual Pride talk could be a foothold for me into the upper leadership of our church. Just to stop the flow of aitches I asked them how last night's meeting went.

Gerald said, 'You should've gone, Dad. It was good. Mostly for married people really.'

Thought how nice it was to see Gerald so serious for once. I said, 'What happened?'

Gerald said, 'Seven couples asked James Dobson into their lives.'

My son will end up as thunderbolt fodder, I swear he will ...

Saturday

Still one blinking 'H' short! Unbelievably, Thynn was here *again!* Ignored all hints. He sat on the floor staring at our goldfish and singing The Green Green Grass of Home over and over again. Anne said there's probably something wrong that we don't know about, but what a pain! How can I work this thing out by tomorrow with Thynn doing Tom Jones impressions all over the carpet?

1.00 am. Still only got two headings beginning with 'H'. Too tired now. I'll get up early and work on it.

Sunday

Church.

Took my Cruden's Concordance to the meeting with me. Went through the aitches secretly during the prayers, still looking for my third heading. Only half realised that Leonard had gone up to the front to give a testimony. Sat up and took notice when I saw by my watch that he was running over the time when I was supposed to start my talk. Glared at him until I found myself listening to what he was saying.

'... and this last week – well, not exactly a week to be precise, more like eight days – it's been very, very thingy. Difficult, I mean, very, very difficult not to err ... not to err ... do it – drink, I mean. Not that it's wrong for anyone else to drink of course – well, it might be if they'd got the same problem as me – but not err ... normally. Where was I? Oh, yes, very difficult over the last approximate err ... week. So every time – nearly every time I felt like going our and err ... abusing my – for want of a better word – body, I went to the Plasses'. Not to abuse my body I don't mean. Good heavens, no! No, I just know they'd never err ... turn me away, as it were, and I could just stay there until the old oojermaflip – the old whatsitsname – the old temptation err ... went away. Nothing like having people who treat you like one

141

of the old thingy – family – know what I mean? Just want to say how, well ... how much I – you know ...'

Realised my third heading was 'Hopeless' – me, I mean. Told everyone that, when I got up to do my (short) talk. Invited Thynn home for lunch afterwards, and thanked him privately in the kitchen for trusting us. He went red and knocked a full bottle of milk onto the floor.

I asked Gerald later what he really thought of James Dobson.

He said, 'Dad, I would go so far as to say that he's a combination of two of the greatest names in the Old Testament.'

I said, 'What do you mean?'

'Ah,' said Gerald, 'you see, James Dobson is an anagram of "Moses and Job".'

Mmmmm ...

I don't really think you've got much to worry about, Andromeda, do you?

Love to you and Lucky Lucy,

From Uncle Adrian.

Dear Madam,

I write to you once again on the subject of toasters in general, and one toaster in particular: namely the electrical appliance which I purchased at your emporium some two or three weeks ago. Now, I am a broad-minded, flexible man, but I have certain stubborn, possibly even prejudiced, views on the ideal function of such machines. My idea, and you may wish to dismiss it out of hand as being wild and fanciful, is that one should be able to place slices of bread into the appliance and, a minute or two later, remove them in a toasted state. An eccentric whim perhaps, but there is a surprisingly substantial body of opinion which freely endorses such a view, and I feel it may be of benefit to you to be aware of this new and revolutionary movement in case other customers in your establishment should purchase similar pieces of equipment and take them home with just such a narrow expectation lodged in their minds. Let me suggest one or two minor refinements that may be thought useful in the particular model with which you supplied me.

At one end of the machine is a small dial, which can be turned from a point marked 'LIGHT' to a point marked 'DARK'. It was in connection with this dial that I made my first error. The morning after my purchase I was obliged to rise at a very early hour before the sun rose and while the temperature was uncomfortably low. Happily, my home is very adequately lit and heated by electric power so I was able to reasonably anticipate a pleasant breakfast in warm surroundings before commencing the day's duties. Having placed two slices of bread into the 'toaster', I then turned the aforementioned dial to 'DARK', and pressed down the lever which, I assumed, would simply lower the bread into the inner recesses of the appliance. How I ever contracted the lunatic idea that 'LIGHT' and 'DARK' referred to the degree of toasting required, I really could not say. But, though I say it myself, I am a fast learner. As the lights went out and the entire electrical system in my house ceased to function, I realised how foolish I had been.

Turning the dial to 'LIGHT', however, did not restore the general illumination.

Much later, and after considerable expenditure on the services of an electrician, my lighting and power were restored, and your machine had been cleverly converted into something approaching the appliance I had originally envisaged. I say 'something approaching' because there are still some very minor improvements that might be possible. May I suggest, for instance, that the terms 'LIGHT' and 'DARK' should be replaced on similar machines with the terms 'NOT TOASTED AT ALL' and 'CREMATED'. Alternatively, and I slip this in merely as a little personal preference, might it be possible to produce a radically new variety of appliance which toasts bread to the degree required by the appliance's owner?

I do hope that you will not feel I am fussing over trivial details, and I look forward with eager anticipation to continuing a dialogue on this subject when I bring your 'toaster' back to visit you later in the week. I should love to hear your views on refunding, or the exchange of faulty goods.

Yours sincerely,

Percival X Brain (Elderly and frail)

P.S. Looking back through my files, I note that I have already written to you twice on this matter. I hope you will not brand me a fanatic. Did you know, by the way, that there is an old tradition, still upheld in some parts of the country, of actually replying to letters?

Dear Geruld,

I have had a letter from your naybour, Mister Brain, ackewsing me of selling him a crabby old toester. I gnow being an attraction mite do funny things to the mined, but shorely I'd rememba if I'd sett up a bizness ~~selling~~ forlty ~~elek~~ elecritdl stuff to old men. Eh? Shorely! Mister Brain mite have got a bit seenile in the head, beeing old and aul. It carn't be easy when yor name is Brain and most of it's gon.

Cood you arsk him to eggsplane pleese, Geruld?

Lucky Lucy says HALLO GERULD.

Logical bonds
Andy-pandy xx

P.S. I've put Mister Brain's loony letter in for you to Peru's. (good werd eh, Geruld. It meens look at).

Dear Andy Pandy,

What a scream! What a panic! What a to-do! Thank goodness you sent me that letter! Bless your little cotton socks, you prevented an innocent man from being dragged off to the cells. It was real drama – just like on the television. I'll tell you what happened. Ready? Okay!

I got your letter telling me about Mister Brain and the toaster after I came home from college the day before yesterday. (I came home at two o'clock in the afternoon, but don't tell Mother – she doesn't think college counts if you haven't been there *all* day.) I went straight round after I'd read it to see old Percy and ask him what was going on. 'Toasters?' I thought. 'Funny!' I thought. Anyway, he wasn't there, so I thought I'd try again after tea. I was going to ask Dad what he thought about it, but I chickened out in the end. Dad's got a heart of gold, but – well, what's the point of complicating things? So, about seven o'clock, I stepped out of our front door to climb the fence to Percy's place. Then I stopped dead, because what do you think I saw standing outside Mister Brain's house?

Well, what do you think?

Come on – have a guess!

You can't? Right! I'll tell you then.

It was a police car, Andy Pandy, with an orange stripe all round it and a blue light on top, sitting there as large as life. For a moment I thought I'd better go back inside and mind my own business, but I just couldn't. I WAS NOSEY!!!! Awful, isn't it, Love and a Dream? God has to forgive me for something or other every single day. (Wish I was perfect like you.)

Anyway! Like I said, I was too nosey to leave it, so I hopped over the fence and up to Percy's back door, which I found wide open. In I walked, all innocent, and through in the front sitting-room I found a scene like something out of a bad play. There were two policemen in full uniform looking all stern and stiff, and standing between them was a lady who – well, she was one of those tall, angular ladies who look as if they've put their make-up on in the dark with a shaving brush. And she was looking *very* angry. All three of them were glaring at Percy Brain as if he was the lowest sort of criminal there was. Now, I don't know if you realise this, but Mister Brain used to be an actor, Andy Pandy, throwing his arms about with a loud voice on a big stage – that sort of thing. He looked just like that now, crouched back against the wall with one hand over his heart, and the other thrust out in front of him as if he was trying to keep vampires away. And his eyes! They were wide and crazy looking, and his mouth was hanging open. He was *really* laying it on thick, was old Percy, but he was a bit worried as well, I could tell. A bit pale and twitchy – know what I mean?

So then this lady held a piece of paper out in Percy's direction, and spoke like someone who's just been chewing on a slice of lemon.

'Do you deny,' she screeched, 'writing this letter threatening to cripple me with your car if I don't give you a new toaster?'

'Threatening? …cripple? …toaster?' gasped Percy. 'I totally, absolutely, categorically deny sending *any* such letter!'

Well, then she read out loud from this piece of paper, and this is how it went.

'Dear young lady,

What an unfortunate accident a broken leg is! The pain must be *very* unpleasant. It is amazing, is it not, how easily such things can occur when we least expect them. Goodness me, you could be immobile in hospital for many weeks with such an injury. Some claim that such occurrences are the consequences of less than virtuous treatment of others, but this is surely not the case. You, for instance, might step into the street and be hit by a car whose driver, for one reason or another, has failed to pay sufficient attention. I, myself, might easily make this kind of mistake. I could make it tomorrow! I intend to visit you *very* soon, so I will not write more now. I wonder if you remember me? I *do* hope so! Look out for me.

Yours in anticipation,

    Percival X Brain.

Yes, you guessed it, Andy! Poor old Percy had got his letters mixed. The lady in the toaster shop got the one meant for you, and you got the one complaining about the toaster. Good job I was on the spot with the other letter, wasn't it? All sorted out in the end. The boys in blue were in stitches – they thought it was hilarious. I got a feeling the lady was a bit disappointed really, though. I think she'd hoped Percy would be taken out and hung from the nearest lamp post. Tried to explain it all to Dad later, but I might as well have tried to strike a match on jelly.

Love to Lucky Lucy and, of course, Andy Pandy,

    Gerald.

PART FIVE

10, Drowning Street,
   London,
   Youknighted Kingdum.

Dear Misses Thacher,
        Have you ever bean an attraction? I doon't think so. Not on the natural helth ennyway. I am pubblickly horizontall and proud of it. I bet you woodn't have yor lemur mended by an uncwollified sturgeon called <u>Mister</u> Fisher. My name is <u>Veal</u> by the way. I leen to the left and I am a bit red. My muther is up with the green and common wimmen and Gwenda, still tryeing too get rid of the crude rissoles. I bleeve you are verry kean on Mister Raygun's base, Misses Thacher, like that man with a nayme that sownds lik a beddtime drink who had an affare with a hellicopter and climed out of the cabinet to sulk after you told him off. Well I'm <u>knot</u>! Why doon't you tell Mister

Raygun to keep his rissoles in his own base? How meny people have to becum green and common befor you see cents? Eh? If I can werk it out with grate weights hanging off my ancles, shorely you can do it vertikal! You havvnt got grate weights on you. Hou is yor son Mark? Father said that Mark Thacher is an ambishun, not a persun. It's the only thyme I ever saw farther and Gwenda agree. Farther spoilt it a bit later when Gwenda said — Arn't you intarested in batterd wimmen, and father said — yes, I'll have two large ones and a dubble porshun of chips pleese.

Annother thing Misses Thacher, can you do sumthing abowt Dugless Nurd's hare? Farther used to say he looks lyke an unhappee ice-creem cone in the wind. Why don't you get Weedwell Sosoon to give him a bit of a trimm? Father said if you stuck a sigar in his ear heed look lyke a 99.

Ennyway, aul I can say is wot abowt a ewe-turn Misses Thacher? If you beecame a soshulist lots of the uther stories mite get a bit less blue. Eh? Mister Kinnerk mite give you a job if you do. Grarnted you woodn't be abul to be Frying Mincer and hav yor own persunnel defective, but you wood at leest avoid beeing infiltraighted when the reverlooshun cums. I am in tuch with Mister Georgeous chops. I cood put in a werd for you.

yors in antissipayshun

Andromeda Veal (Mizz)

P.S. Witch one is yor persunnel defective? Is it the one with gray hare and glasses?

Global One-man Evangelism Movement
International Drag-a-Pew Project
Prefab Number 3
Armistice Row
Bagshot

Telephone   (Decided not to reconnect after scripture revealed
             it was visiting 'friends' who ran up the huge bill.
             Jeremiah 12:6 'They have called a multitude.')

Dear Brother or Sister,

Please excuse the hand-written pink crayon on shiny toilet paper, but when Stanley left the Project with my other assistant, he took his John Bull printing set with him, and I have run out of paper bags.

As you will note from the new project title, a revelation has once again been vouchsafed to me, and we are, in obedience, setting out on a new course. When I say 'we', I mean in fact 'I'. Like Gideon of old I have seen the fearful and the kneelers removed from my midst, and I alone am continuing the work set before me. Stanley and Bruce are singularly lacking in vision and adaptability. Stanley in particular seeming to surrender to a spirit of moroseness after his unfortunate experience at the Frog and Spittle on amateur night. I reminded him that there are worse fates than being covered with beer by a drunken audience intent on making a fool of you because you tried to play the spoons with only one spoon and no experience whatsoever, but he appeared unconvinced. Bruce was infected by this negative attitude to such an extent that when I announced the termination of the musical project they were both unripe for change, and decided to leave.

The new, and certainly most exciting project to date, will involve the hauling of a thirty-five foot wooden Victorian church pew through every country in the entire world, on foot. Preparations are complete, other than details such as finding a suitable pew, talking its owner into giving or selling it to me, working out how to move it, planning a route, sorting out passport and visas, amassing sufficient finance for the journey and selling the prefab. Once again I am absolutely determined that this will be a faith venture, and already I have received a firm offer of the loan of a screwdriver as and when I locate a suitable pew. I regard this as strong confirmation of guidance received thus far.

Over the last week or two I have been touring the local churches speaking to groups about my unwillingness to publicise the project purely for the purpose of raising much needed capital. I always take with me a pile of the sort of financial pledge form that I do *not* want filled in by those who are seeking only to salve their consciences. I enclose such a form with this letter. Please strike out either 'I give willingly to the Lord,' or 'I intend to keep my money for my own selfish pleasures and I don't see why God should get his hands on it,' then sign the form and return it to me. Please do *not* feel pressured to respond in a particular way.

Yours,

Vernon Rawlings (sic sec)

P.S. A fresh revelation this morning. Clear indication from scripture that I should sail my pew like a raft around the oceans. Ezekiel 28:2 'I am sitting on the seat of God, surrounded by the seas'.

P.P.S. Please pray for a paddle.

Dear Rabbit Runcie,

    I am a non-anglian attraction cauled Mizz A. Veal. The onley uther one of yors I gnow is the Neverend Boom who has a bit of trubble soughting out what's a dimmonimation and what's a brekkfust serial. Rest ashored I have aulso written to the Pope abowt mayking babys do the limbo and that, so I'm not just gettting at yew Rabbit old chapp. My frend Geruld (his persunnel problum is the onley thing that's maid beeing horizontall beardabull) says yor name is a nammagranamm of C. E. but in error, so he mus lyke you two. Eh? One thing yor lukky abowt is yew doon't have to be a halibut like my frend Farther John at the nunkery or the Pope in his Fattycan, but I have a fealing yor not quyte asin charje as the Pope. He can say wot he lykes withowt feer of contraception from the catlicks eeven if the car-

diggans get stroppy, but yew have
to mayke speechis at a speshul
plaice cauled the Sinodd. My
frend Geruld says it's maid up of
sum peeple who've been ordrained,
lyke beacons and curits and shot-
guns and bish ups and rectums,
and the rest are drorn from the
~~the~~ Layertee (whoevver they mite be
when there at home, eh Rabbit?),
but they aul have to be peeple who
lyke to Sinodd, and evvrywon
torks and torks for ajes and ajes
and then decides to leeve evvrything lyke it wos befor. Sounds a
bit of a waist of thyme to me,
Rabbit, but I eggspect you gnow
best beeing the arch bish up.
    Ooh, Rabbit! I wish I'd been
yew marreeing Prints Charls and
Laidy Die! I saw it on a film.
I gnow they are bluddsukkers on
the tyred flesh of the British prola-
dairyfat, but I think their acey-
pacey skill and aul. I lyke the
~~queen~~ queen two, eeven tho I'm not
aloud to rearly. Shee nearly cryed

when thay got married by yew,
diddn't she? Wozzn't it nice of
the inshorance cumpany to lend
you their bilding for the day? I
 hope you wrote them a thancyou
letta. Did you Rabbit? It's only
plite.

   Rabbit, wot is a bish up? It
sownds lyke a missteak of sum kind,
but why do yew keep mayking new
ones if that's wot they are? Wot
woz aul that fuss abowt the
Durrem one who said things abowt
the verging berth and the west
direction of Jesus? He is a bish up,
isn't he? He is cauled the bish
up of Durrem, lyke the Grate fyre
of London, eh?   I think he looks
nyce, but praps he shood have
stuck to sprinting.

   Ennyway, wot I wonted to arsk
woz, sumtimes when yor going up
and down the Lambuth Warlk,
cood yew just remined God that
Andromeda is waiting with a unknit
lemur for a bitt of actiun green
and common wummen - wise?

Good on yer, Rabbit! Lucky Lucy
says thancyou two. She is my first
dolly sins Bigot, and I am heaping
her eeven if I lern the wrong
roll in serciety.
     Logical Bonds to you
        and aul the bish ups,

           Andromeda Veal (Mizz)

P.S. My frend Geruld says his nice
fashist dad's car must beelong to the
Cherch of England becos it onley
goes in for a service twyce a year.
Goodun', eh?

P.P.S. If yew and the Pope beleeve
in the same God wot's so speshul
abowt cantering through
Walkerbury Catheedrul togetha?
      Eh?
    For goodniss sake!

Dear Andromeda,

Gerald says you very much enjoyed the last extract from my diary that you saw – the bit about my talk on Spiritual Pride – and that you wouldn't mind seeing some more. I'm *very* pleased that you enjoy my diary so much. I sometimes think that Gerald, and even Auntie Anne sometimes, don't really understand that you can learn things from experiences recorded in this way. I have known Gerald to sit with tears of laughter running down his face whilst reading an entry that doesn't appear even remotely humorous to *me*. Still, he's a good, kind lad, so I don't really mind.

By the way, I'm really pleased you liked your doll. We went right through two shops before we found one that looked right. We had to leave the first shop we tried because the manageress foolishly took offence at some perfectly innocent remarks I happened to be making to unsuitable dollies, but in the end we met Lucy and all agreed that she was the one. We *did* enjoy leaving her

161

on the pillow beside you. Dear Andromeda – I felt so sorry for you stuck in that bed for so long. I'm glad you think I'm a *good* fashist now. I hope I'm good. I do try, but I seem to get in such a tangle sometimes. When I wanted someone to do the chairs at church for instance. It was really … well, that's the bit of the diary I've put in for you to look at. Hope you find it interesting.

Monday

Edwin, our Elder, rang to ask if the study group I lead could take responsibility for putting out the chairs at church every Saturday evening ready for Sunday. I said, 'No problem, Edwin!' Felt rather proud of my 'team'.

Phoned Stenneth Flushpool and asked if he'd do it. He said he'd commit it to the Lord in prayer, and ask his wife. Gerald was listening. Said that if God and Mrs Flushpool disagreed he wouldn't put much money on God's chances.

Tried Richard Cook next. He said that it was unscriptural to make definite plans for the future, so he couldn't promise to do it every week, but 'as the Lord leadeth'. Asked him how far in advance he reckoned the Lord might let him know each time. He said, 'It is not for us to know, but may your faith be equal to the test, Brother.'

I have discovered that you can't strangle telephones …

Tuesday

Vernon Rawlings (one of my study group) gave a talk tonight at the monthly church meeting about sacrificial giving. Very strong and inspiring. So impressive I started making notes near the beginning. Last bit went as follows:

'… and let's face it, brothers and sisters, when we talk about giving we usually mean parting with a small part of our surplus. We pay lip service to the Christian ideals of love and charity, but when it really comes to the crunch, are we ready to give freely and cheerfully beyond the point of comfort? Are we, brothers and sisters? I want to ask you all …'

Vernon pointed dramatically at various members of the church as he went on in a loud voice.

'... young Christian boy! Young Christian girl! Brothers and sisters of middle age! Elderly friends! I want to challenge you right now! Are you prepared to give until it hurts? Are you prepared to take what you have in terms of money and possessions and time, and give whatever is needed to whoever needs it, or are you just going to play at religion by keeping the best for yourself and throwing a few scraps to your neighbour? I challenge you tonight, brothers and sisters! The next time someone comes up to you and asks you to give or do something, will you deny your faith and say "NO!", or will you count the cost and, despite personal expense, say "YES! I'll do it!" '

Collared Vernon straight afterwards and asked if he'd do the chairs. He said, 'No, I'd rather not. There's good telly on Saturday.'

Wednesday

Stenneth Flushpool rang. Said he had no inner peace about the chairs, and he wouldn't be allowed to do it anyway.

Richard Cook rang. Said he now felt that the Lord would have him stand with me in prayer about the chairs, and would that do?

Tried Percy Brain. He said that when I'd tried everyone in the entire universe and still wasn't able to get anyone, then he *might, possibly* help *very* occasionally, but that would depend on circumstances at the time, so it was better to rule him out other than *very, very* exceptionally. And even then he couldn't promise.

Thanked him for sparing the time to talk to me ...

Sat down by the telephone and rang *all* the others. Never heard such a load of feeble, pathetic excuses in all my life. Bit fed up with my 'team' by the time I finished. What a list!

William Farmer: Bad leg, which for some lunatic reason means he can't use his arms.

Leonard Thynn: Chairophobia (?)

Norma Twill: Didn't want to spoil the sensitive soft skin on her hands.

Ephraim Trench: Said he'd disagreed with buying this particular set of chairs thirty-seven years ago, and his integrity would be in question if he was seen to be helping with them now.

Raymond Pond: Said his ministry was in music, not chair arranging, and could I ask whoever *did* do it to stay well away from the organ please?

Honestly!

Thursday

Study group tonight. At the end I really stormed at everyone about the chairs. Pointed out that *no one* had offered to help.

'And because of that,' I concluded, 'we all know who's going to end up doing the chairs every Saturday evening – Anne!'

After they'd all gone off looking very subdued, Anne said, 'Darling, I didn't want to say anything in front of everybody, but I don't quite understand why I'm the obvious choice to do the chairs.'

'What do you mean?' I said, a little shocked.

Anne said, 'Well, why shouldn't you do it, for instance?'

'Don't be silly,' I said, 'you know Saturday's the night when I always like to – ah, I see what you mean ...'

Friday

Good job I'm a Christian. If I wasn't I'd tot up all the things I've done for my study group members and send each one a bill. As it is I naturally forgive them freely for being so selfish.

Saturday

Gerald offered to come down with me to help with the chairs this evening. Surprised to find the front door left unlocked. Even more surprised to find nearly all of my study group inside! They'd turned up to help with the chairs! Organised a rota for the future and got on with it.

Norma wore gloves.

Ephraim supervised.

Thynn kept his eyes shut.

William hopped.

Gerald spent the entire time working out that Alex Buchanan is an anagram of 'Ex-banana hulc'.

Went home feeling quite warmed inside.

So you see, Andromeda, it all got sorted out in the end. It usually does. It's the sorting out bit that seems to get complicated. When I get to heaven I've got a few questions to ask God ...

Love to Lucky Lucy and you,

Uncle Adrian.

P.S. Why don't you work out an anagram for Gerald's name? I did once. I think he was quite impressed. By the way, your Uncle Edwin's planning to come and see you tomorrow.

Dear Andromeda,

After visiting you last night I've decided to write to you because I'm afraid you might be getting a little confused. Mind you, I don't blame you! With everything that's happened to you and your family I would be surprised if you hadn't got things a *bit* upside-down.

As you know, Andromeda, I'm the Elder at my church and I think most of the people who go there think I'm not too bad at the job, but nearly all of them reckon I've one main fault. I wonder if you can guess what it is. You're *very* good at saying exactly what you think, so you might find it rather hard to understand! My problem is that I hardly *ever* speak out loud and clear about what I think and believe. People think I should do it much more often (especially when they think someone else has gone wrong!), but I just carry on in my own way most of the time – people who've got problems or aren't quite sure about things seem to find it easier to get close if I don't make too much noise. After talking to you last night though, I thought I ought to be more 'LOUD AND CLEAR' than usual. You see, I know how angry and upset you must be about your mother and father going off and leaving you at a time when you need them so much, and I'm sure I'd feel exactly the same. I just want to say one or two things to you. First, there's nothing wrong with what your Mum's doing. She believes very strongly in what's happening among the protestors up at the missile bases and we need people in this country who are willing to do more than just *talk* about things being wrong. I admire your Mother very much, and I think very highly of your Dad too. He just got fed up with not feeling very important, and started saying unkind things and making the kind of jokes that he *knew* would upset your Mum and Gwenda until things got so bad that he had to leave. Now, I know it sounds as if I'm just having a go at your parents, but it's only because I can remember just the same thing happening to me. You see, when your Auntie Joan and I moved down here and I took over the eldership of a church for the first

166

time, I made the same sort of mistakes that I think your Mum might be making. I was quite young and very anxious that everything should go really well in the church, and it never occurred to me that Auntie Joan and our two little girls needed me at home just as much or more than most of the people in the church. I was out just about *every* evening, Andromeda, doing what I thought of as 'The Lord's Work', and if I'm really honest, I quite often made sure that 'The Lord's Work' started just before the time when the girls had to be bathed and put in bed and read to. I was never there, Andromeda! And if anyone had said to me, 'Do you love your family?', I'd have got very stiff and indignant and said, 'What *do* you mean? Of course I love them – I'm a church Elder!' I didn't understand you see. I came to my senses in the end when someone wise and kind gave me a bit of a telling off, but it went on for quite a long time, with poor Auntie Joan just having to put up with it because every time she complained I said that I was only doing what God told me to do. The things I was doing were good and useful and all that – it's just that I didn't realise (or didn't let myself realise) that there were even more important things to be done in my very own home. Maybe that's what's been happening with your Mum, Andromeda. There's no doubt she loves you, and your Dad's potty about you – always has been. I think they just let things go too far and get too bad, and in the end neither of them could stand it, so away they went, leaving you in the middle, sweetheart. It happens to an awful lot of children I'm afraid. But don't give up. I haven't. Your Mum and Dad were always great pals underneath everything and my guess is that they probably still are. Keep badgering God, and so will I.

Your loving Uncle Edwin.

Dear Andromeda,

Victoria (Mrs Flushpool) has asked me – well, told me – I
should write you a letter. My name is Stenneth Flushpool and I am
married to Mrs Flushpool (Victoria). You may be a little puzzled
by my name. I am called Stenneth as the result of a disagreement
between my parents. At my christening the vicar asked in which
name I was to be baptised, and my father replied, 'Kenneth'.
Simultaneously, my mother, a rather dominant lady, not unlike
Victoria (Mrs Flushpool), replied 'Stanley'. The Vicar, an elderly
man with somewhat impaired hearing, interpreted this confusion
of sounds as the word 'Stenneth', and baptised me accordingly.
My parents decided to accept this accidental compromise in the
interests of peace, and I have been Stenneth ever since. I cannot
say it has been a happy accident for me. There is invariably a short
pause when I am introduced to a new acquaintance, while the
person concerned controls his or her features and deals with the
rising gust of mirth which the mention of my name always seems
to precipitate. Do you find my name amusing?

However, enough of that. Victoria (Mrs Flushpool) was of the
opinion that the bulk of my letter to you should consist of rel-
evant and instructional verses from scripture, together with helpful anecdotes of testimony from my own life. I am not, however,
bound to abide by the wishes of Mrs Flushpool (Victoria). It has
been suggested that I am unduly influenced and even dictated to
by Victoria (Mrs Flushpool), but this is not wholly the case. Last
week, for instance, I was adamant that I would select my own new
pinny for work in the kitchen. It is essential to win these battles
from time to time. But I digress. The fact is, Andromeda, that I
was myself obliged to remain in hospital for a long period in traction some four years ago. In my case it was a back problem, but
I did experience all the same physical discomforts and indignities
that you are undergoing now, and I would like you to know that
you have my deepest sympathy. I would also, if you do not mind,
like to share a confidence with you that I have shared with no

168

other person, and particularly not with Mrs Flushpool (Victoria). You see, despite all the discomfort, I really rather *enjoyed* my stay in hospital. It was not unlike an extended holiday. Many of the nurses who cared for me were pretty, friendly girls, and I experienced a most unusual sense of specialness whilst lying so helplessly in my bed. Naturally I was *deeply* conscious of the absence of Victoria (Mrs Flushpool), but she did visit every other day to read lengthy extracts from holy literature for the whole of the visiting period. I find it difficult to express my appreciation of such devotion. On those occasions when she was not present though, I indulged myself in two areas, of which, I fear, Mrs Flushpool (Victoria) would not have approved. First, I managed to persuade one of the porters (a Mr Blogg if I remember rightly) to bring me some magazines on model aircraft construction, an activity which Victoria (Mrs Flushpool) regards (I believe mistakenly, though I say nothing) with some suspicion. These afforded me immense satisfaction, but it was my other activity that occupied most of my unvisited time. (Why I should be writing all this to a young person like yourself, I really could not say.) My other activity arose out of my dissatisfaction with my name – Stenneth. I spent very considerable periods simply imagining that my name was Kirk C. Flushpool (the C stood for Craig). Most of these imaginings were in the form of dialogue between myself and a new acquaintance. Here are some examples:

NEW ACQ: Hello, you're a fine looking chap. What's your name?

ME: Kirk, actually.

NEW A: What a great name! What's your middle name?

ME: Craig.

NEW A: My name's only Paul. I wish I was called Kirk Craig!

ME: They're only names. Paul's nice.

This is one I used to pretend was a telephone conversation from work.

ME: Hi! Flushpool here, K.C. Flushpool. Do you want to buy some of our goods?

CUSTOMER:	That name sounds terrific! What does the K.C. stand for?
ME:	Only Kirk Craig. Very ordinary names really.
CUSTOMER:	Ordinary names my foot! They're great names, and I bet you live up to them.
ME:	Oh, I don't know.
CUSTOMER:	Well, look, Kirk ...
ME:	Yes?
CUSTOMER:	I'd like to put in a really big order, as long as it's you who handles it. Okay, Kirk?
ME:	Sure thing! Kirk out.

This must appear very foolish to you, Andromeda, but I enjoyed these little pretendings very much indeed, and I still think about those weeks in the ward sometimes, although I do not mention such things to Mrs Flushpool (Victoria). I fear she would not understand.

Do forgive me for writing a letter that seems, now that I look back at it, mostly about me, but I have greatly appreciated the opportunity to express myself a little on paper. I do hope you are soon well enough to return home.

Yours sincerely,

Stenneth Flushpool.

P.S. Please bear in mind when/if replying that Victoria (Mrs Flushpool) is not aware of the contents of this letter. I do not intend deceit, but unnecessary upset would be rather unfortunate.

P.P.S. Please do not think that I am not sympathetic with Mrs Flushpool (Victoria). I think that if we had been able to have the child that we both so much wanted, she would have been a lot less – stern.

Dear Mister Flushpool, (It wood be districtspeckful of me two caul you Stennith).

Thankyou for yor letta. The scrippcher versis and anicdotes were rearly grate! Acey-pacey eggsiting and good four me and aul. (Nudje, nudje, wink-wink, eh?) Pleese give my rigards to Misses Flushpool (Euston), and say that I wood be pleesed to see her ennytime, eeven if I'm asleep. In fact if shee's thinking of cumming to kindely read me lencthy eggstracts from holey lichrercher, it wood be betta if I was asleep becos sientists say you can lern a lot in yor brain wile yor asleep. Eh? I think so.

By the way, I arsked Mr. Blogg if he remembered you when you were in here. He said — O yes, that bloke wot wanted magazeens about scripcher and that brort in, he wos orlright he wos — so he does rememba you Mister Flushpool. (I cept my fingas crossed while I wrote the bit abowt the maga-

zeens, Mister Flushpool) Mr. Blogg
can burp wenever he wants to by
the way. I wish I cood burp wenever I wanted to. Pleese inquire
of yor wife whether she can burp
wenever she wonts to. Tell her yew
have to be carefull it cums out
the rite end.

Ennyway, that's aul for now from
yor frendly littal horizontall
attraction.

Logical Bonds
Andromeda

P.S. I doon't think Stennith is a
funnee name (just in case you wundered
wether I thort it was) I think it's a
sweet nayme. I think yor rather sweet,
Mister Flushpool, axshully.

P.P.S. If yew shood happen to meat an
old frend of mine cauled Kirk Craig
Something-or-other, cood you tell
him how mutch I like his names?

P.P.P.S. Perhapps Misses Flushpool
(Paddington) will have a lot less

stern as thyme goes by. It wos
sad wot you wrote larst. Nevver
to have a George. Eh?

Dear Geruld,
        Gess what! If I spell
yor name aul wrong with a
A instead of a U, yor a
nammagranam of —

   SLADE SPRALG!

Goodun, eh? It makes you
sownd like a acey-pacey
weerdo film star.
        By the way, Geruld. I
thort I'd just menshun that
it's my berthday next friday.
I'm not remineding you in
case youd forgottun you were
going to give mee a brand new
persunnel problem aul of my
own, Geruld. I'm just men-
shuning it in passing. I
doon't mined if you forgett
to give me one
        Logical bonds (to Sladey-baby)
        Andy-Pandy X

P. S.   It's this friday cumming
when I doon't mined you
forgetting to give me a brand
new persunnel problem. aul of
my own, Geruld. The one just
cumming up at the end of
this week.

P. P. S. Thanckyou for lending
me your persunnel problem
aul this time (like what I
havvn't got one of my own of).

Dear Andy Pandy,

Hi! It's Slade Spralg here. How's tricks? Now listen carefully my little love and a dream – or read carefully rather – because I'm putting my life in your hands. If Dad finds out I've sent you this bit of his diary there's likely to be another attraction down your way soon. One called Gerald. You see, Dad doesn't come over all that dignified in this extract from his great classical work. Mind you, he doesn't come over all that dignified in *any* of his entries, but this one is – well, you read it and see. And if you see Dad coming – eat it!

Monday

Why did God let cars be invented? Nothing but trouble and expense! In all the Christian paperbacks people travel fifty miles with no engine and four flat tyres almost every other day, just by the power of prayer. My cars have all been unbelievers. They sigh and give up. Even when *I* think they're okay someone else thinks they're not. Like this morning. Took my perfectly good car up to Ernie Pavement, our Christian mechanic, for its MOT. None of us has ever seen Ernie laugh. When Gerald told him we wanted a fully charismatic gearbox fitted in our last car, he said he didn't stock them. That's what made this morning so upsetting. He started by walking slowly round, staring sadly at it like someone watching a close relative die. Then, before I could tell him what I wanted, he patted me gently on the shoulder and suggested in a low, mournful voice that I should just walk quietly away without looking back and he'd see to its disposal.

I said, 'No Ernie, it's a perfectly good car! I don't want it disposed of. I want you to put it through its MOT.'

That's when he started this dreadful grating, helpless laughter. Ended up hanging over the bonnet wiping tears from his eyes with an oily rag. Good job for his sake the grease gun wasn't a couple of feet nearer my hand.

Gritted my teeth. 'Well, at least LOOK at it!' I said.

He walked round it again, poking bits here and there, and making clucking noises with his tongue, then he said, 'Looks like a resurrection job, mate.'

Asked him what he meant.

He said, 'Needs a completely new body.'

Went home very depressed (although inwardly rejoicing on some deep level of course). Wondered how I'd ever be able to afford a new car. Prayed about it, and suddenly in my mind's eye saw a brand new Volvo Estate!

Claimed it.

Tuesday

Saw fleets of new Volvos in my dreams all night. Told Anne over breakfast that I felt we were being led into praying for a brand new Volvo Estate, but she displayed what to my mind is lamentable faithlessness.

She said, 'Let's be realistic, darling. We're looking at something small, economical, probably second or third hand and easy to park.'

Gerald stopped overeating for a moment to offer to sell us his old skateboard if we wanted it. Stupid boy!

Told Anne that I was going to believe for a new Volvo Estate. She said she thought it was much more likely to be something like a ten year old Datsun. We agreed that we'd each look for confirmation between now and Saturday.

Wednesday

Extraordinary! Everywhere I go the roads seem to be packed with Volvos. Counted twenty-three. A real sign!

When Anne came home she said she'd seen *twenty-four* Datsuns. Bit of a blow really ...

Thursday

Counted eighteen Volvos today. Anne's score was thirteen Datsuns. I'm winning by four Volvos on aggregate! I don't like to doubt Anne, but I find her claim that she's hardly noticed any Volvos on the road very hard to accept. On the contrary. I don't understand where all these Datsuns appear from. I can't recall seeing *any*.

Friday

Excellent Volvo crop today. Anne went one better with her ridiculous Datsuns, but I'm still winning overall.

Leonard Thynn round tonight. You can always tell when Thynn thinks he's got something funny to say. He tries to look cool. Told me part of my car problem is solved because he's found a scripture verse in which God promises to arrange transport home from work for believers. Asked wearily which one it was.

He said, 'Isaiah, chapter twenty-two, verse nineteen. "I will drive you from your office".'

Thynn and Gerald cackled away like parrots. Left them cackling. Thynn borrowed the cat without asking while I was upstairs. Asked Anne tonight what he does with our cat. She looked surprised and said, 'That's just what I was going to ask you, darling. I thought *you* knew.'

One of these days I shall follow him ...

Saturday

Saw THIRTY-FOUR Volvos today! Absolute famine of Datsuns.
Hurried home to announce final confirmation of my leading. Anne
arrived just after me. Said she'd seen seven hundred and sixty-three
Datsuns! Turns out Gerald took her over to the Datsun factory by
bus. Gerald said, 'Is that guidance, or is that guidance, Dad?'

Was just about to accuse them of cheating when Ernie Pavement arrived at the door. Said sadly that he'd found a car for us.
Escort. Five years old. Good nick. Only one problem – the heater
didn't work. Quite cheap. Did we want it?

Went for a drive in our new car later with Gerald. Saw no end
of Volvos *and* Datsuns. Curious!

Car went well. Terribly cold though. I felt like a lump of fro-
zen meat. Must get the heater fixed. Gerald pointed out that Old
Escort is an anagram of Coldstore.

Feel a bit embarrassed about all that Volvo counting. Hope
God wasn't watching – well, of course he *must* have been watching, but I hope – well ...

What Dad doesn't realise, Andy Pandy, is that there never was
a trip to any Datsun factory, and Mum never really kept a tally of
Datsuns she saw on the roads. She was just kidding Dad along till
he came out of his latest loony phase. Dear old Dad! He's a rather
sweet old fashist, don't you think, Andy Pandy?

By the way, I happen to know why old Leonard borrows the cat.
It's very ingenious really. You see, he turns on his reel to reel tape
recorder, and then – well, I'll tell you about it when I visit next. It's
not the sort of thing you can describe properly in a letter.

Give my love to Lucky Lucy and Rosy Roundway. See you
soon.

Love, Gerald.

P.S. I'm just off to the shops to buy something for a friend's birthday.

P.P.S. Eh?

Dear Andromeda,

Exciting news! Your Mum rang last night to say that she's travelling down late on Thursday evening to be here for your birthday on Friday. She tried to ring the hospital but kept not getting through to the ward, so she rang us instead and asked if I would pass the message on. Oh, darling, I'm *so* pleased Mummy will be with you on your special day. She'll be on her own by the way. Gwenda's got engaged to a man who writes comedy for Channel 4, so she won't be protesting for a while. I've never heard your Mum sound so excited. She's really dying to see you, sweetheart.

By the way, Gerald will be popping in just for a few minutes on Friday to bring you – well, wait and see! Uncle Adrian and I will come over with our presents on Saturday if that's OK, so you'll have two birthdays really, won't you? And when you come out of hospital at last, you poor old thing, I think we ought to have a really nice late birthday party for you. What do you think?

We're still praying for you, Andromeda.

See you on Saturday.

Love, Auntie Anne X

Dear Andybugs,

I didn't *know* you were in hospital. Edwin contacted me last night. I honestly didn't know that you'd come a cropper and got laid up for so long. Everything went out of my head when I left home and I've just been working without stopping since then in a sort of daze. Andybugs, you do know that your silly old Dad loves you, don't you? Just because I went away doesn't mean I don't care, sweetheart. The other day at work someone asked me if I'd got any children, and I was about to be all grumpy and say mind your own business, when I suddenly saw you in my mind and felt really proud. 'Yes,' I said, 'I jolly well have got a child. She's the finest little girl in the whole world, and she's called Andromeda.' You *are* the finest little girl in the world, sweetheart, and Mother and I have done the rottenest job in the world looking after you. But maybe it's not too late to try. I don't know.

Listen, Andybugs. I can't get to you for a couple of days, but I'm on my way. I shall see you on Friday. OK? Save a big kiss and a hug for me. I'll be coming through that door to see you very soon, and I'm not going to go so far away ever again. Keep your chin up!

Love and kisses,

Daddy X X X

P.S. I haven't forgotten what day Friday is, love!

Dear God,

Don't do enny big relevash-uns or angel cwires or that because I'm writing this in the middul of the night with a torch (not eesy when yor horiz-ontall, God). or Nurse Roundway will tell us both off. Being God won't help yew if yew annoy Nurse Roundway, God! Shee's a wholly terrer when she's rowsed. That's why I'm writing this in a whissper. The rest of the ward's aul quiet, but I'm too eggsited to sleep. Gess what, God? I gnow you gnow ennyway, but I want to tell yew what's going to happen on friday. Farther wrote me a letter, God! He did! He did! He wrote me a letter and cauled me Andybugs and said he'd come on friday and oh, God, issn't it eggsiting! And it's dubbly acey-pacey brill eggsiting because mother's cumming on friday too! Oh, God, I'm a bit fritened about them seeing eech other. Oooh, I go aul tingly when I think abowt it! Enny chance of yew beeing here to reff the match, God ? It is my birthday on friday, you know. Eh?

Ennyway, I'm going to try to go to sleep now. Do you sleep or are you bizzy sorting out Ostralia all night.

I'm glad I got to gnow yew.

Goodnight, God

Logical bonds,

Andromeda Veal (Mizz).

THE THEATRICAL
TAPES OF
LEONARD THYNN

This book is dedicated to:
Matthew, Joseph, David and Katy.

*Who put up with their father's bad temper
when he is trying to write funny stuff*

Dear Reader,

Sometimes I wish I'd never collected Andromeda Veal's letters together for publication. You wouldn't believe how many people from the church have mentioned 'casually' that they've always thought their lives would make a good book. Vernon Rawlings, for instance, who's got a prefab down in Armistice Row and changes his ministry like other people change their socks, approached me with the modest suggestion that I should write his biography and entitle it *Miracle Man – The Vernon Rawlings Story*. He said he thought it would be good if the person who designed the cover made his name look as if it was carved out of massive blocks of stone. I said I'd think about it, which was a lie.

Mrs Flushpool, on the other hand, informed me regally that she was prepared to accept my assistance in the composition of a 'most important spiritual work' to be called: *Crossing the Carnal Swamp* or *Escape from the Natural*. She added that her appointed spouse, Stenneth, would contribute lengthy footnotes as he was one who, since his regeneration, had never been sucked into the bog. This was no more attractive a proposition than George Farmer's offer to supply material for a worship leaders' manual with the title: *Spontaneous Worship and How to Organise it so that it Happens the Same Every Week*.

Much more constructive, it seemed to me, was an idea put forward by Gloria Marsh, an attractive widowed lady who attends our Bible-study group from time to time. Gloria sat very close to me on the settee one evening, and said she'd been looking through her old diaries and letters and wondering if she might have some material worth publishing. She asked if I'd like to come round for a few evenings and look through her bits and pieces to see if there was anything I fancied. Anne, who must have been listening through the hatch, refused this invitation rather abruptly on my behalf. I felt that this was somewhat presumptuous and probably unscriptural. After they'd all gone, I asked Anne what was wrong with providing a little comfort to a lonely soul. She said, 'It's not her soul I'm worried about ...' Ah, well, perhaps she's right. She usually is.

Richard Cook, round to visit one evening, said that he thought it would be a good thing to produce Christian periodicals to combat the pernicious effect of the girlie magazines that you can see (if you look, which he doesn't) on the top rack in newsagents' shops. Gerald suddenly became animated. 'Yes,' he said, 'you're right, Richard. We could publish our own magazines!'

'What would they be called?' asked Richard, stepping goofily over the precipice as usual.

'Well, one could be called *Prayboy*,' said Gerald earnestly.

Richard's mouth was hanging open to the size of a golf ball.

'And then we'd have *Amen Only*,' continued Gerald, 'and how about *Repenthouse?*'

Richard almost needed the kiss of life to jerk him back into the land of the living, and we nearly lost him again when Gerald asked if he'd be willing to remove his glasses for the centre-fold. I don't know what Gerald would do without Richard to act as his straight-man.

Richard's son, Charles, wrote to me from Deep Joy Bible School to suggest that I help him with a book he felt he had to write, and which would change the face of Christian outreach as we know it. The title was to be *How to Communicate that which has been Vouchsafed to us by He Who Would Have us Share that which we have Received Through the Mighty Working of His Eternal Will, in Everyday Language, by One Empowered to Make an Open Profession of Faith to Those Who Have Ears to Hear.*

'A catchy little title,' said Gerald when he saw it.

There was also a request from Percy Brain for me to read what he described as a 'Lawrencian short story', written by his second cousin's nephew's best friend's aunt on several sheets of grease-proof paper with a blunt pencil. Percy said he wanted me to be absolutely honest about what I thought of it, because his second cousin's nephew's best friend's aunt wanted good constructive criticism and not hollow flattery. As far as I could decipher, the story was about a crowd of very odd people saying inexplicable things to each other during a sea voyage on a liner. It was full of lines like: 'She was deeply curious about her own liver ...' and

'She fell into his chest ...' At the end of the story the five main characters all fell into the sea at the same time, and found each other's true selves in a joyously deep act of drowning. When I suggested mildly to Percy Brain that his second cousin's nephew's best friend's aunt might need to do a little work on her manuscript before it was ready for publication, he revealed that, in fact, *he* was the author of the story. He said that if he had known he was to be viciously harangued by a jealous so-called fellow-author, he would never have allowed me to see what one of his closest and most unbiased friends had described as 'a modern classic'. He refused to speak to me for a fortnight.

It certainly never occurred to me that Leonard Thynn would have anything worth publishing. The only thing I'd ever seen him reading (apart from the Bible on church weekends – everyone reads the Bible on church weekends) was *The Good Pub Guide* and the *Beano*. Then, a few months ago, he invited Anne, Gerald and me round for the evening to listen to some tapes he'd made. I'd forgotten that he'd recorded most of the meetings and rehearsals leading up to the Christian drama festival that our church contributed to last year. He even recorded the evening itself, which is interesting because ... well, you'll see for yourself as you read on. It was I who directed our 'presentation', and it was such a hectic business that I hardly noticed Thynn's infernal machine revolving away constantly.

Anyway, after listening to all the tapes, Gerald and Anne persuaded me that this was something that should be shared with the world. I wasn't quite so sure, not least because I didn't exactly come over in the most dignified light. Thynn got so excited though, and Gerald and Anne were so sure that it would help other church drama groups (in a 'negative' way, whatever that might mean), that I gave in and agreed to transcribe and edit the tapes. I do hope it was a good idea... .

Yours Truly,

Adrian Plass.

ONE

HOW IT ALL GOT STARTED ... AND ALMOST ENDED

After an announcement during church one Sunday, that we hoped to enter the local Christian drama festival in a few weeks' time, this meeting was intended to be a brainstorming session. All were welcome, and as free refreshments were provided, thirteen people came. Edwin, our elder, suggested that I should take the chair.

[*Tape commences with a succession of crackles and hisses as Thynn's tiny brain wrestles with the complexity of a switch that is labelled in big red letters: PRESS TO RECORD.*]

ADRIAN PLASS (A.P.): Right, well we'd better get started. We're meeting this evening to discuss ...

THYNN: *(Interrupting.)* Hold on a sec.! I don't think it's recording. *(More crackles and hisses.)* Yes it is. Sorry! Carry on.

A.P.: We're meeting this evening to discuss ...

THYNN: Wait a minute – the little red light's not on. I'm pretty sure the little red light ought to be on. I don't think it's record-ing. Yes it is! No it's not! Wait a minute. *(Tumultuous crack-les and hisses and thumps, together with unseemly words muttered by Thynn under his breath but clearly audible on the tape.)* Right, I'll just do a test ...

A.P.: *(With rather impressive patience.)* Leonard, old chap, we really ought to ...

THYNN: *(In a high-pitched, unnatural voice.)* Testing, testing, one two three testing! This is your sound sound-man testing for sound. One two three, I'm L.T., this is a sound test, testing for sound. One two ...

A.P.: *(With slightly less patience.)* Leonard, I really think ...

[*Sound of machine being switched off, followed by sound of machine being switched on again.*]

THYNN: There you are, it was recording all right after all. Let's get on. It's late already.

A.P.: *(Through his teeth.)* We're meeting this evening to discuss the ...

THYNN: Could we just wait while I run the tape back to the beginning? There's no point in ...

[*Sounds of a chair falling over and a forest of crackling and hissing as A.P. goes over to strangle Thynn. Repenting at the last moment he whispers in his ear instead.*]

A.P.: *(Hissing murderously.)* If you don't shut up about your tape recorder, do you know what I'm going to do?

THYNN: *(Nervously curious.)* What?

A.P.: I'm going to thread the tape up one of your nostrils and pull it down the other.

THYNN: *(After a moment's consideration.)* Fair enough. *(In normal tones.)* I don't think there's much point in running the tape back to the beginning. I'll just start recording from here.

[*Sounds of* A.P. *picking his chair up and sitting in his place again. Very faint sounds of* THYNN *whispering 'waste of tape' to himself.*]

A.P.: Right! Good! Perhaps we can get on now. We're here this evening to discuss ...

MRS FLUSHPOOL: *(Interrupting.)* I realise that I am not the chairman of this meeting, but do you not feel that supplicatory cover is a fundamental requirement at the commencement of a Christian endeavour such as this?

[*Puzzled silence.*]

ANNE: *(Sitting next to me.)* I think Mrs Flushpool means that we ought to start with a prayer, darling.

A.P.: Oh! Err ... yes, of course. A prayer. Right! Err ... would anyone like to ... ?

CHARLES COOK: *(Back from Deep Joy Bible School the day before.)* Shall I ... ?

A.P.: Yes, Charles, go ahead.

CHARLES: Okay, let's just turn away from the hurly burly and the rush and bustle and the every-day concerns and the toing and froing and the ups and downs and the worries and the problems and the responsibilities and yesterday's regrets and today's anxieties and tomorrow's fears and ...

A.P.: *(Loud throat clearing noises.)*

CHARLES: ... and let's just get into that peaceful state where we're just ready to just receive and just listen. Let's just keep silence for just a minute while we just err ... do that.

193

[*A minute's silence during which Charles can be heard making little smiley sipping noises with an occasional isolated 'just' escaping like air from a slow puncture in a bicycle tyre.*]

... we just want to just ask that this thing we're going to do – I can't remember just what it is just at the moment – just that it will really be just really blessed in a way that's really just right and that we'll all be really conscious of how you just want to really help us to just do it in the right way and that all those involved will just really come to know that you just want to just really show them how you really just want them to just realise the truth about just understanding that you're really err ... just.

GERALD: *(Leaning over to whisper in my ear.)* If you don't stop him soon, dad, we're going to just have three choruses and just a call to the front before we just get started.

CHARLES: So we ask that we'll just really know your will and really just be really encouraged – oh, hallelujah! *(He starts to sing.)* Bind us together ... !

A.P.: *(Loudly.)* Amen!

[*A volley of 'Amens', ranging from the half-hearted muttering of Thynn, still preoccupied with his machine, to Vernon Rawlings' manic cry of 'Amen! Hallelujah! Bless you, Lord! Oh, yes, amen indeed!'*]

A.P.: *(Wearily.)* We're meeting this evening to discuss what our contribution to the ...

ANDROMEDA VEAL (A.V.): *(Here with Uncle Edwin.)* I'm afraid I don't find that very funny.

ANNE: *(Sensing my imminent breakdown.)* What don't you find very funny, darling?

A.V.: What Mrs Plushfool said about Uncle Adrian bein' the Chair*man*.

MRS F.: *(Sitting up very straight, like a water bed standing on end.)* My name, child, is Flushpool, not Plushfool ...

A.P.: Oh, for goodness sake ...

194

MRS F.: ... and I fail to see how a mere child such as yourself could have any comment to make on my remarks to the chairman.

A.V.: That's why I intersected – insurrected – indisected – said what I said just now. He's not a chairman, he's a chair*person!*

MRS F.: May I say, in love, little girl, that, in my view, the feminist movement is almost certainly contrary to scripture. I myself am under the authority of my husband, Stenneth. *(Sharply.)* Confirm that please, Stenneth!

STENNETH F.: Eh? Oh, yes, dear. Absolutely. Whatever you say ...

A.V.: And can I say in love, Mrs Slushpoof, that I wish you'd go and live on the Isle of Person, or anywhere really, and ...

ANNE: That's quite enough now, Andromeda. You mustn't be rude. Please stop laughing, Gerald. It doesn't help!

EDWIN: *(Mildly.)* Let's just say that we call Adrian 'Chair'. All agree?

[*Chorus of assenting murmurs.*]

A.P.: *(A pale shadow of himself.)* We're meeting this evening to discuss ...

THYNN: Could we go back to where you said 'Oh, for goodness sake'? The little red light wasn't ...

A.P.: *(Stands and flips his lid.)* All right! Okay! Fair enough! Let's not talk about drama. Let's talk about tape recorders and little red lights and what I ought to be called, and let's pray great long prayers and say things to each other in love! Let's not do what we came here to do! Let's completely waste our time and then eat all the food and then go home! *(Sound of a body slumping back into a chair.)*

[*Silence.*]

ANNE: *(Soothingly.)* Everyone's listening now, darling.

A.P.: *(Quietly grim.)* We're meeting this evening to discuss what our contribution to the local Christian Drama Festival ought to be. This is a brainstorming session, so I'll just write down all the ideas everyone has, then we'll discuss which is the best one to use. That's all – it's quite simple really. Quite simple. It really is.

THYNN: Excuse me, Chair ...

A.P.: *(Very calm.)* If this is about your tape recorder, Leonard, I shall commit grievous bodily harm on your person.

THYNN: No, no it's an idea – for the festival.

A.P.: *(Guardedly.)* Yes?

THYNN: Well, it's about this man, right? He's an alcoholic, dependent on drink. Drinks all the time. First, we see him sitting at home drinking. *(Continues in a low, dramatic voice.)* He takes one drink, then another, then yet another until the bottle is empty. In the next scene we see him with a bottle of vodka. Again he drinks it glass by glass. He bemoans his fate and cries aloud for help. In the third scene, just as he drinks the last drops from a bottle of rum, he's converted, and everything's all right!

[*Pause.*]

A.P.: And may I ask, Leonard, who you thought might selflessly abandon sobriety to enact this moving piece of drama?

THYNN: Well, I thought as it was my idea, I should ...

A.P.: I thought so. Next!

THYNN: But ...

A.P.: I've written it down. Next!

PERCY BRAIN: *(In resonating theatrical tones.)* I believe I may lay claim to more theatrical experience than that of this whole company combined. I have considered the matter with great care, and I know what we must do. It shall be an epic! The entire history of the Holy Bible will unroll across the vast wooden plain of the stage. In scene after magnificent scene, we shall depict the gigantic forces of creative energy flinging the sun into its place on the black cloth of heaven, the making of man and his Fall, the construction and journeying of the mighty Ark through the floodwaters of divine punishment, the tragic tale of the kings and prophets of Israel, the misery of Egyptian captivity, the parting of the waters of the Red Sea, the tale of

Daniel and the gigantic image before which he would not bow, the birth, life and death of our Lord, the imprisonments, ship-wrecks and mighty deeds recorded in the Acts of the apostles, and finally, superbly, cataclysmically, the visions, the battles, the judgments, and the final days of this planet, as pictured in the book of Revelation!

A.P.: It's going to be a bit hard getting all that into ten minutes.

RICHARD COOK: And we've only got thirty-one pounds, sixteen pence in the entertainment budget.

EDWIN: And we can't have proper scenery because of the different groups coming on and off stage.

GERALD: And the vast wooden plain of the stage is actually ten blocks pushed together.

A.P.: And we haven't got enough people for that sort of thing anyway.

THYNN: Apart from that it was a jolly good idea, Percy. *(Laughs immoderately.)*

PERCY: *(Glaring at me as Othello glares at Iago in the last scene.)* Am I to understand that the scenario I have laid before you is to be rejected with the same sneering contempt with which you flung a previous manuscript back into my poor smarting face ... ?

A.P.: *(Firmly.)* I never flung anything back into your poor smarting face, and we haven't rejected your ideas, I simply tried to point out that ...

PERCY: I sensed no carping reluctance in your manner on that occasion when you requested the loan of my excellent mechanical hedge-trimmer. Is that act of generosity and open-heartedness to be forgotten so swiftly? With what grief I echo the poet's words: 'There might I see ingratitude with an hundred eyes gazing for benefit, and with a thousand teeth, gnawing on the bowels wherein she was bred ... !' *(Rests his head on his arms as if grief-stricken.)*

[*Depressed pause.*]

A.P.: Yes, well – can we get on? Has anyone ...

MRS THYNN: *(Turning her hearing aid up.)* Can I ask a question?

A.P.: *(Warily.)* Yes?

MRS T.: When are we 'avin' the food, and why 'ave we got to call you Claire?

ANNE: *(Kindly but loudly.)* Not 'Claire', Mrs Thynn. Edwin said we should call Adrian 'Chair'.

MRS T.: *(Groping for comprehension.)* But that's sillier than callin' 'im Claire! Why 'ave we got to call 'im Chair? No one's called Chair!

A.P.: *(Almost shrieking.)* It's short for Chairman, Mrs Thynn! I'm the chairman you see!

MRS T.: Well, why aren't we callin' you Chairman then?

A.P.: *(Shrieking.)* Because Andromeda thinks we shouldn't be sexist!!

MRS T.: Why're we takin' any notice of a scrap of a girl tellin' us we shouldn't exist? Anyway, when's the food?

A.P.: *(In a little, hoarse, broken voice.)* Leonard, could you please convey to your mother that no one gets anything to eat until I get some ideas down on this piece of paper? That is what we are here for.

198

PERCY: *(Finding his grief ignored.)* Blow, blow, thou winter wind, thou art not so unkind ...

GERALD: ... as Claire's ingratitude to Percy.

VERNON RAWLINGS: *(Preventing infanticide by interrupting.)* Err ... Charles and I have got something, Chair. We sat up late last night and worked it out. It's a sort of thing for sort of Christian outreach. It sort of came to us in a surge last night, just like it must have been in the upper room, although we were actually in the basement not that it matters, because whichever room ...

A.P.: What was your idea, Vernon?

VERNON: Yes, well, we thought we'd write something sort of gritty and real that would really glorify the Lord and bring a mighty blessing to everyone who sees it, didn't we Charles?

CHARLES: Yes, we really just ...

VERNON: We thought we could start with the drama festival and then move to one of the provincial theatres, and go from there to the West End before doing a year-long international tour, didn't we Charles?

CHARLES: Yes, we just really ...

VERNON: And last night I had a dream that mightily confirmed the leading we felt! In my dream I was a dolphin performing in one of those aquarium places, and the trainer was brushing my teeth with a giant toothbrush! Wasn't he, Charles?

CHARLES: Well, I wasn't really just there ...

A.P.: I'm afraid I don't really see ...

VERNON: *(Very excited.)* Surely it's obvious! The performance bit's about acting – the stage, you know. The trainer's God, and he's symbolically purifying the fish – that's me, for the task ahead.

GERALD: What I don't quite see ... apart from the fact that you do look a bit like a dolphin, Vernon, is why you should appear as a creature like that?

VERNON: That's the really *great* part of it, isn't it, Charles?

CHARLES: Yes, it's really just ... !

VERNON: The fish is a symbol of Christianity!! Amen?

CHARLES: Halleluj ... !

A.V.:*(Dispassionately.)* A dolphin's not a fish. It's a mammal.

VERNON: *(Carried away by enthusiasm.)* Well, what's the difference ... ?

A.V.:The diff'rence is that fish've got cold blood and gills and fins. Mammals are aminals that *(with relish) give suck* to their young. I done it in a project while I was an attraction in hospital. So there!

VERNON: *(Slightly irritated.)* Well, dolphins *look* like fish!

A.V.:P'raps God doesn't know the diff'rence between fish and mammals. P'raps he's forgot, seein' as it all started millions of years ago.

MRS F.: It *all* started, as you so irreverently put it, child, six thousand years ago, and ...

EDWIN: Come now, Victoria, don't be too dogmatic with the child ...

A.V.:*(To Vernon.)* Why don't you ask God to do another dream tonight with you as a haddock. Haddocks are real fish, aren't they, Charles? And you look more like a haddock.

CHARLES: *(Completely confused.)* I just really don't really just ...

A.V.:Mind you, I've never heard of haddocks performing in public.

MRS T.: Why're we talkin' about performin' haddocks, fer Gawd's sake? I thought we was choosin' a play!

THYNN: Sort that lot out, Claire!

A.P.: The next person who calls me Claire is neither going to be in the play, nor have any food.

ANNE: Come on, dear, it was only a joke. Don't be childish.

A.P.: I wasn't being childish – I was just ...

MR F.: I think we have a fundamental doctrinal issue to settle before we proceed any further. This child ...

A.P.: Anyone who insists on settling fundamental doctrinal issues isn't going to be in the play or have any food either.

MR F.: *(Nobly.)* Victoria will never allow threats or promises to affect her defence of scriptural puri ...

MRS F.: Be quiet, Stenneth.

MR F.: Yes, dear.

PERCY: Alas, the gratitude of man, hath often left ...

A.P.: Anyone misquoting bits of poetry about ingratitude gets no part and no food either.

[*Pause.*]

Right! *Please* can we get on. Vernon and Charles – never mind about the dream. Just tell us what your idea is please.

VERNON: Okay, well basically it's one chap talking to another chap in a pub. We thought a pub was sort of better, because it's sort of real and – well, real, and if there's anything we want to be, it's real, so we thought it ought to be in a pub, so that it's real.

A.P.: *(With grinding patience.)* Yes? And ... ?

VERNON: One chap's a Christian called Dave and the other's a non-Christian called Bart, and they have a really natural sort of conversation about sort of faith, don't they, Charles?

CHARLES: Yes, it's really just natural, just like a really natural err ... conversation.

VERNON: We'll sort of do what we've sort of written, shall we? It's not long enough yet, but we can easily sort of pad it out when – if we err ... need to. I'm Dave, right? And Charles is Bart, aren't you, Charles?

CHARLES: Yes, I'm really just Bart.

[*Rustle of scripts.*]

VERNON: Right, well it starts with Bart sort of sitting on his own in the pub, sort of talking to himself. Right, Charles, whenever you're sort of ready. *(Whispers.)* I come in soon, but not sort of at the beginning ...

CHARLES: *(Much clicking of the tongue and sighing.)* Blow! Huh! *(Sigh.)* I don't know! My life isn't going very well! I have had three big beakers of alcohol already this evening, and I shall probably have a lot more before I go home. Huh! *(Sigh.)* Blow!

What is life really about? If only I could see some meaning in it all. I see no reason not to sin at present. I have a good mind to smoke a cigarette and be naughty with a lady. No wonder people such as I turn to a life of crime. Rootless and ignorant, we go around with the wrong sort of chap, not realising that with every step we move farther from God, about whom we know nothing. Barman, I hereby order another shandy, and I don't mean the children's sort! *(Click, sigh.)* Huh! Blow!

VERNON: *(Sounding like Baden-Powell addressing a Scout rally.)* Good evening, friend. May I sit at your table with you? I will not force my company on you, as that frequently produces a resentment that hardens the listener to attempted impartation of the gospel.

CHARLES: Something about your sensitivity attracts me, sunk though I am in the misery of godless self-absorption. Sit down if you wish. But – I say, you are a laughable person. Is that not a glass of orange squash in your hand? Ha-ha, you are not a man of the world as I am. I am on my fourth beaker of shandy, but – huh – who is counting? *(Sigh.)*

VERNON: I count it a joy to suffer your mockery, friend. I require no base intoxicant to produce the joy that springs from within. Can you not tell from the expression on my face that I draw from other wells than these? *(He smiles a ghastly, crinkly smile.)*

GERALD: *(Leaning over to whisper in my ear.)* If anyone smiled at me like that in a pub you wouldn't see me for dust ...

A.P.: Sssh!

CHARLES: Now that you mention it there is an almost visible aura of joy, peace and contentment about you. To what do you attribute this phenomenon?

VERNON: No, no, friend, let us talk first about your life and work, your hobbies and interests. In this way we shall establish an easy, natural relationship – a platform on which to build a friendship that is not exclusively concerned with the welfare of your soul. Scripture supports this method of approach.

CHARLES: I am a welding person, recently made redundant. Life does not seem worth living to me at present. Blow! Huh!

(Sighs.) I have been sitting here all evening attempting to drown my sorrows through the medium of alcohol. I have already consumed three beakers of this devil's brew. It is shandy, and I don't mean the children's sort. But enough of me. Now that we are close friends and you have shown yourself interested in me as a person and not just as a form of spiritual scalp, tell me the origin of the love, joy and peace that flows from you like a river.

GERALD: *(Whispering again.)* Yeah! What's he put in his orange squash?

A.P.: Sssh!

VERNON: As you ask me, friend, I shall tell you. I am a Christian, and the joy that you witness is a product of redemptive suffering, apprehended through divinely implanted spiritual vision, nurtured and developed through appropriately organised exegetical study.

CHARLES: I have never heard it explained so simply. Oh, that I too might share this simple faith. *(Sighs.)*

VERNON: But you *may* share it, friend! You may indeed! You must choose now between shandy and God. Choose God and you will become as I am.

GERALD: *(Another whisper.)* Back to the shandy then, I guess.

A.P.: Sssh!

CHARLES: I abhor thee, devil drink! I choose God! *(Pause.)* The feeling of joy that I am suddenly experiencing is at once more powerful and subtle than that induced by the excessive consumption of shandy, even though it's not the children's sort. Thank you, friend, for your words.

VERNON: *(Smugly.)* Not I, friend, but he who speaks through me.

CHARLES: And what now, friend?

VERNON: Well, there's a Bible study on Monday, the church meeting's Wednesday evening, Thursday there's a new nurture group starting – you'll need to get to that. Friday night there's a coach going to hear John Wimber, Saturday there's a day-long conference on next year's mission, and Sunday it's service in the morning, Azerbaijanian meal at lunchtime, and communion in the evening.

CHARLES: Free at last!

[*Sound of two people clapping. It is Vernon applauding Charles and Charles applauding Vernon. A short silence follows.*]

VERNON: *(With shy pride.)* Well, that's it. What do you think?

A.P.: *(Clears throat.)* It – it – it's certainly very ...

VERNON: *(Anxiously.)* You don't think it's too sort of street-level? Charles and I were a bit worried that it might be a bit too sort of street-level, weren't we, Charles?

CHARLES: Yes, we were really just a bit worried about err ... that.

A.P.: No, I err ... don't think you need to worry about that.

VERNON: *(Slightly hopeful.)* You don't think it comes over too raunchy and realistic?

A.P.: *(As if considering carefully.)* No, no, I wouldn't say that at all.

ANNE: *(Kindly.)* You must have both worked very hard on it I expect, didn't you?

CHARLES: Well, we just really felt that God had really just given it to us.

GERALD: *(Whispering in my ear.)* Glad to get rid of it, I should think.

A.P.: Ssh! Okay, well what did other people think?

EDWIN: Good effort. Jolly good effort! Not perhaps quite what we ...

PERCY: As I understand it, there are a mere two characters in this – 'effort', as Edwin so eloquently describes it. Are the rest of us to be 'pub extras'? If so, I strongly prot –

A.P.: *(Quite gratefully really.)* That's a very good point actually, Vernon. As Edwin said, it's a very good – a very good – a very good err ... effort, but it does only involve two characters, so it is just a little bit limiting. Anyway, we know it's there if we want to ...

GERALD: *(Whispering.)* Put on something really bad.

A.P.: ... if we want to come back to it later. Now, Gerald *(thinking to teach him a lesson),* how about you? Have you got anything to offer?

GERALD: Funny you should say that, dad. *(I might have known.)* As it happens I have prepared a little scene. Not quite as Pinteresque as Vernon and Charles' err ... effort – more sort of observed behaviour rather than anything to do with outreach and that sort of thing.

A.P.: What sort of 'observed behaviour'?

MRS F.: *(Grimly.)* I trust we are not about to enter the realms of your accustomed flippancy, young man.

GERALD: *(Gravely sincere.)* Thank you, Mrs Flushpool. I appreciate that.

MRS F.: *(Bewildered.)* What are you thanking me for?

GERALD: For your trust, Mrs Flushpool, for your trust. Thank you for trusting me.

ANNE: That'll do, Gerald. What's your idea?

GERALD: Well, basically, it's a couple of typical young Christians meeting in one of the restaurants at one of the big Christian holiday events like 'Let God Spring Into Royal Acts Of Harvest Growth' or something like that.

A.P.: Typical young Christians?

GERALD: Yes, more or less.

A.P.: Go on then.

GERALD: Well, there's Gary. He comes from *(puts on a voice)* 'a really great fellowship in the Midlands – really lively and the gifts are used, and the pastor's written three books, and we have some really great speakers, and two of my best friends have come through in the last six months, and we've just started a prophetic basketball group, and last week we claimed Greenland for the Lord, and next year a group of us are going over there, and we've had lots of prophesies about ice melting and the summer going on right through the winter, and I'm trying to decide whether to be a full-time evangelist or a Christian scuba-diver and my prayer partner said he sees me immersed in water so I think that's quite clear guidance really, and I'm reading a great book at the moment called *Origami and the Christian – a Frank Look at what the Scriptures say about Paperfolding,* and some of us are going to go and hold up posters outside the local stationer's next Friday, and I've just written a devotional song with G minor seventh diminished in it, and ...'

A.P.: *(Amused but nervous.)* And the other one?

GERALD: Well, about the same really, except his name's Jeremy and he's not sure whether to be a full-time Christian entertainer or a charismatic accountant. Anyway, this is how it goes. I'll have to do both parts myself because I haven't practised it with anyone. It starts in the middle of their conversation.

Jeremy: ... so I thought it would be great to join O.M. *(Casually.)* I had a chat with Ishmael about it last time he was up.

Gary: Oh, do you know Ish?

Jeremy: Oh, yeah, Ian's a good friend.

Gary: Nice house – nice place to stay.

Jeremy: *(Defeated.)* You've stayed there, have you?

Gary: Well, err ... no, not exactly stayed as such, but I've heard that it's a nice err ... place to stay.

Jeremy: *(Relieved.)* He's great though, isn't he?

Gary: Oh, yes, he's great!

Jeremy: So what are *you* going to do?

Gary: Well, I think I might be being led to spend some time with YWAM. I heard all about it from a chap who works for C.L.C. Bumped into him up at C.B.C. when I was working for S.U. He's an A.O.G. who used to be an R.C. Made the move after a B.Y.F.C. rally.

Jeremy: Impressive, was he?

Gary: Not initially. He was introduced to me by a bloke from L.S.S.

Jeremy: Are they sound?

Gary: And light, yeah. Anyway, after this chap had talked about YWAM for a bit I really felt I was being led in that direction, so I took the whole idea to Elsie and talked it through.

Jeremy: What's that stand for?

Gary: What does what stand for?

Jeremy: L.C.?

Gary: It doesn't stand for anything. It's my girlfriend's name – Elsie.

Jeremy: Oh, I see!

Gary: What's that stand for?

Jeremy: What does what stand for?

Gary: O.I.C.?

Jeremy: Nothing, I was just …

Gary: Only joking! Anyway, after talking about YWAM to this chap …

Jeremy: The R.C. who became an A.O.G. after going to B.Y.F.C.?

Gary: Yes, that one. After talking to him and Elsie I really felt led to go and work with old Floyd again.

Jeremy: Old Floyd? You mean Floyd McClung? You mean the one who wrote that book – the one with the brown cover?

Gary: Yes, that's the one. That was a great book, wasn't it?

Jeremy: That was a *great* book!

Gary: A *truly* marvellous book.

Jeremy: Mmmm … what a book!

[*Reverent pause.*]

Gary: You've err … you have read it, have you?

Jeremy: Well – flicked through it, you know … You?

Gary: Not read it, no, but everyone says it's err …

Together: A great book!

Jeremy: What did you mean about 'working with Floyd again'?

Gary: *(Airily.)* Oh, we did a mission together a couple of years ago, that's all.

Jeremy: You and Floyd McClung did a mission together?

Gary: Well, afterwards he said he wanted to personally thank me for the support I gave him – actually he said he wanted to personally thank about a hundred and twenty of us for the support we gave him, but I always felt he gave me a special look, so …

Jeremy: Actually, I'm really into the music side of things lately.

Gary: Yes, I've just used G minor seventh diminished in a …

Jeremy: It would be great to play keyboards with someone like Martyn Joseph.

Gary: Who's he? Friend of yours?

Jeremy: *(Shocked.)* He's one of the top performers at Let God Spring into Royal Acts of Harvest Growth and Blackbelt …

Gary: Blackbelt?

Jeremy: Yes, it's like Greenbelt only better. Martyn's always there. He's *great!*

Gary: I think U2 are absolutely superb.

Jeremy: *(Deeply moved.)* Well, thank you very much! I didn't realise you'd heard me playing. Do you really think …

Gary: I said 'U2' not 'you too'. I was talking about the band called U2.

Jeremy: Oh, yeah! U2 are *really* great!

Gary: Born again Christians …

Jeremy: Really sort of secular as well …

Gary: Great music on any level …

Jeremy: Great how they don't act like non-Christian bands …

Gary: That Bono …

Jeremy: The things he says ...

Gary: Really sort of honest and unhampered ...

Jeremy: Not like a Christian at all ...

Gary: *(Sings.)* '... I still haven't found what I'm looking for ...'

Jeremy: Great!

Gary: Great!

[*Pause*]

Jeremy: Not quite sound?

Gary: Not quite. We've found what we're looking for, haven't we?

Jeremy: We have? I mean – we *have!* Anyway, I must go. I'm meeting a girl who's here with CYPAS over by the E.A. stall. We're having tea with a U.R.C. couple who've just done a tour with M.F.O. in Africa. She's hoping to go to L.B.C. while he gets a couple of months in with W.E.C.

Gary: I think I'll have a sleep.

Jeremy: Okay, R.I.P.

Well, that's it! What do you think?

EDWIN: *(Chuckling softly.)* Extremely amusing, Gerald, but I don't somehow think it would go down too well at the local festival. They do take themselves rather seriously.

VERNON: *(Clearly puzzled.)* Of course, it's really good, Gerald, but err ... I didn't sort of see it as funny. I mean, it was really sort of two ordinary Christian chaps having the sort of chat that, well, that we young Christian chaps have, wasn't it?

A.P.: Surely people don't really talk like that! I can't believe ...

RICHARD: Of course they don't! We were only saying on the SPUC committee the other day, or rather a chap from SPCK was saying, that in all his years with the WCC and SASRA before that, how sensible and mature Christian conversation is, whether you're in the YMCA or a school C.U. All that stuff about initials was, frankly, completely O.T.T.

A.P.: Mmm ... yes. I see what you mean, Richard.

GERALD: I know an A1 S.R.N. with a B.M.W. and the sweetest B.T.M. you ever ...

ANNE: Gerald!

PERCY: *(Sniffing.)* Discussion is superfluous. We have already established, or I believed we had established, that a duologue is not suitable. Unless of course *(fixing A.P. with an accusing eye)* we are being abused by a nepotist!

MRS T.: *(Straining to hear.)* Who's bin bruised by a methodist? Doesn't surprise me, mind you …

A.P.: *(Raising his voice.)* No one's been bruised by a methodist, Mrs Thynn! Mr Brain thought I might be favouring Gerald's idea, because he's a relation!

MRS T.: I thought we wasn't doin' Revelation, like old 'Enry Irvin' over there suggested.

A.P.: *(Bawling.)* We're *not* doing Revel … !! Oh, never mind, Leonard, explain to your mother please.

PERCY: I will not be referred to as 'Old 'Enry Irvin' over there'!

MRS T.: Well, come an' sit over 'ere! Then you can be Old 'Enry Irvin' over 'ere!

PERCY: I have *never* been so … !

MRS F.: I am very much afraid that Gerald's little piece of non-sense embodies those elements of flippancy and irreverence that seem to characterise the greater majority of his utter-ances. I fear, Mr Chairman, that there is an undue residue of the natural in your progeny.

EDWIN: Victoria, this really is not the place for …

A.V.: She said 'Chairman'. She was s'posed to say 'Chair'! Some-body pass a motion – quick!

PERCY: To think that I, who once trod the same boards as – as – as Peter Butterworth, should be subjected to …

MRS T.: Peter Butterworth! Now yer talkin'! *(Laughs shrilly.)* 'E was in all them Carry On films, wasn't 'e? 'E was good, but my favourite was …

MR F.: *(A strange rasping laugh.)* I very much enjoyed the perfor-mances of that charming fair-haired girl who always seemed to have very large parts.

[*A profound silence falls. During it, Mrs F. turns with ominous slowness to look at her spouse.*]

MRS F.: I was not aware, Stenneth, that you had attended *any* of those highly questionable presentations.

MR F.: *(Even his voice is pale.)* Ah, well ... yes, well ... of course ... that was – was before we were err ... married, my dear. Before you err ... assisted me in seeing so clearly that err ... almost everything is err ... wrong, as it were.

MRS F.: *(The air is heavy with 'Wait till I get you home'.)* Mr Chair ...

A.V.: *(Interrupting with triumphant precision.)* ... person!

MRS F.: I would like to move ...

THYNN: Hear, hear!

MRS F.: I would *like* to move that none of the suggestions received so far be adopted. They are either ungodly, unsuitable, or incompetent.

GERALD: *(Whispering.)* And there isn't a part for her.

A.P.: Ssh! Look, could we just ... ?

[*There is a lot of loud noise as someone crashes through the door and slams it shut behind them.*]

ELSIE BURLESFORD: *(For it is she – out of breath, but not energy.)* Hello, everybody! Hello, dad! Sorry I'm late. William and I have been at the back of the fruit shop rebuking China and doing our maths homework. William believes we can actually change the shape of countries through prayer and he's read about someone in South America who's actually chipping bits off Peru, and he doesn't see why it shouldn't happen here, and neither do I, so we're going to ...

GERALD: It's a great idea, Elsie! We wouldn't need ferries to get to the Isle of Wight any more. You and William can just stand on the mainland and pray the island to and fro all day. Brilliant!

ELSIE: Don't be silly, Gerald. Anyway, I hope I'm not too late, Mr Plass, because ...

MRS T.: You 'ave to call 'im Wardrobe, love.

ELSIE: Wardrobe?

A.P.: *(Shouting.)* Chair, Mrs Thynn! Not wardrobe!

MRS T.: Well, I knew it was furniture ...

ELSIE: Chair? Oh, Chair! I see! Short for chairperson?

[*You can hear Andromeda grinning.*]

A.P.: Elsie, have you got ... ?

ELSIE: *(Great rustling of paper.)* I've brought my idea along. It's a poem! I thought different people could read different verses. I've got them all here; they've got the names on. Each person represents a part of God's creation, you see, so we'd all stand in a line on stage and read it out verse by verse. What do you think?

A.P.: Well ...

ELSIE: Let's try it out! Mr Flushpool, you're first. Here's your verse. Off you go.

MR F.: *(Much throat-clearing. He begins to read at last in a very small, nervous voice.)*
> A lion I, a fearsome beast
> I'm six feet long or more,
> My teeth are white as tennis shorts
> Oh, tremble at my roar.

(Makes a tiny mewing noise.)

MRS F.: Roar, Stenneth! Roar!

MR F.: *(Makes a loud mewing noise.)*

ANNE: *(Whispering to A.P.)* I say, darling.

A.P.: Yes, what?

ANNE: *(Still whispering.)* It just occurred to me that with Stenneth, Victoria and you all sitting in a line, we could do 'The Lion, the Witch, and the Wardrobe'! *(Dissolves into silly giggles.)*

A.P.: Sssh! Err ... that was very impressive, Stenneth. I could just see you stalking the plains ...

MRS T.: Why's 'e walkin' to Staines?

THYNN: Be quiet, mother. Err ... Adrian?

A.P.: Be quiet, Leonard. Carry on Elsie, please.

ELSIE: Right! Mr Brain, you're next. It's on that piece of paper I just gave you. Start when you're ready.

PERCY: *(Declaims in a mountainous voice.)*

> An earthworm, I, a humble worm,
> Of negligible brain,
> I swallow little bits of earth,
> Then spit them out again.

(Sound of rustling paper as he searches for more.) Is *that* my part? That fragment of absurd doggerel? Is that *all*?

ELSIE: *(Undaunted.)* Yes, Mr Brain, it is. And it's not absurd doggerel. William's pretty sure that it's inspired verse. He's just been reading a book about a man in South-east Asia who's written fifteen full length Christian novels despite having been blind, deaf and dumb since birth. William says the things I've written are amazingly similar to the things this man's written.

GERALD: *(Whispering.)* That figures!

PERCY: Humph!

A.P.: Sssh! Not you, Percy, I was talking to Gerald.

ELSIE: *(On the warpath.)* What *did* Gerald say, Mr Plass?

A.P.: It doesn't matter what Gerald said, Elsie. Let's just carry on.

GERALD: I said ...

A.P.: Be quiet, Gerald!

THYNN: Adrian?

A.P.: Be quiet, Leonard!

VERNON: This chap in South-east Asia sounds really sort of ...

ELSIE: Be quiet, Vernon! Now, the next one to read a verse is Mrs Flushpool. Here you are, here's yours. You're an oak tree.

MRS F.: *(Quite flattered.)* Well, I must say that seems eminently suitable. Now, let me see ... *(She begins reading in ringing tones that slow down to incredulity as she takes in the words.)*

> An oak tree I, my arms held high,
> In postures wild and cranky.
> My feet beneath the stubborn sod,
> My skin all brown and manky.

(Pre-natal silence.)

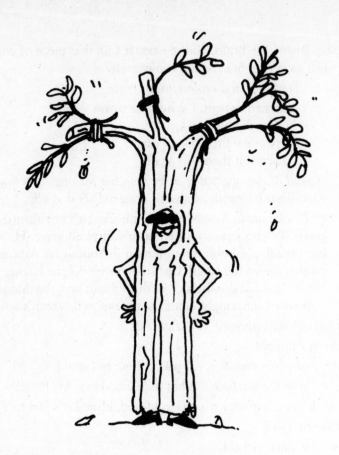

GERALD: Eat your heart out, Wordsworth.

A.P.: Sssh! Elsie, I'm not quite sure ...

MRS F.: *(Faintly.)* Stenneth, defend me!

MR F.: Err ... yes, of course, dear. Err ... I think Victoria is a little upset at the err ... idea that she has been considered physically appropriate for this particular verse. Her skin, after all, is not brown at all ...

MRS F.: Stenneth!!

MR F.: Or err ... indeed err ... m – m – m – manky, and we – we insist on having the err ... *sod* removed, and replaced with turf, or indeed g – g – g – grass.

ELSIE: *(Vocal hands on hips.)* I was led to write those words and I refuse to change a single one!

GERALD: *(Whispering.)* Stubborn little turf, isn't she?

A.P.: Sssh! Elsie, this just isn't working, is it? Perhaps ...

THYNN: Adrian, there's something ...

A.P.: Be quiet, Leonard!

ELSIE: *(About to boil.)* Very well! If you don't want what I've written, I'll tear it all up, and I'm very sorry to have bothered you! William says that we'll thrive under persecution, and I suppose this is the beginning of it. This meeting is like – like – Rumania! *(To A.P..)* I wrote a verse specially for you, Mr Plass, and you don't even want to hear it! William's just heard about a man in ...

A.P.: *(Surrendering.)* All right, Elsie! I'm sorry, I'm sorry, I'm sorry! I will read the verse you wrote for me and then we really must get on. Okay?

ELSIE: *(Slightly mollified.)* Well, all right then. Here it is, and you won't be all sensitive like Mrs Flushpool?

A.P.: *(Testily.)* Of course not! I shall just be objective.

ELSIE: Right, off you go then.

A.P.: *(Reads quite quickly.)*

> A slug am I, a slimy thing
> I crawl upon my belly,
> Behind I leave a sticky trail,
> My body's like a jelly.

[*Round of delighted applause.*]

ELSIE: What do you think, eh?

A.P.: *(Objectively.)* Why the blue blazes do you think I'm specially suited to read that? What is it about me that suggests a slug? I'd just like to know, Elsie!

ELSIE: Well, it had to be someone fat and humble and useful, so ...

A.P.: *(Gritting his teeth.)* Right! That's it! Thank you all for coming! Thanks for your suggestions! Thanks for anything I've forgotten! Nothing's suitable, so we might as well all just eat all the food and clear off! If I'd had any idea that ...

THYNN: Err ... there's something ...

A.P.: What?!

THYNN: It's this. This script.

A.P.: By you? I'm not interested in ...

THYNN: No, it's by FRANK BRADDOCK. He popped in this morning and said could I bring it along because he couldn't get to this meeting. He said it's exactly ten minutes long, it's in rhyming verse, and it's about Daniel in the lions' den. It's got six characters including the narrator and the lions and he wrote it specially for us to do.

[*Long pause while* A.P. *stares at* THYNN.]

A.P.: *(Quietly but menacingly.)* Let me get this straight, Leonard. You have been sitting there with this script, by a proper writer, in your pocket, throughout this farcical meeting, during which people have been told they have manky skins, and bellies like jellies, and I have had to listen to hour after hour ...

ANNE: *(Mildly.)* Less than an hour, darling ...

A.P.: ... nearly an hour of unusable material; and now, only *now* do you produce something which might have saved us all that trouble. Is that a fair summary, Leonard?

THYNN: Err ... let me see ... yes, yes, that's about it. I – I forgot I'd got it, you see. *(Laughs hoarsely.)*

A.P.: Well, in that case I'm going to ... *(sound of chair legs scraping and a little scream from Thynn's throat.)*

ANNE: You're going to forgive him, aren't you, darling? Aren't you, darling?

A.P.: *(Breathing heavily and noisily through his nose.)* Yes! That's it – that's what I'm going to do to you. I'm going to forgive you, Leonard *(Barely audible muttering)* – right in the teeth ... *(Sits again.)*

ANNE: Is the play good, dear?

A.P.: *(Rustling of pages.)* Looks great! Just right. Listen to this bit:

Down in the den on the bone-strewn floor,
Where the lost men scream and the lions roar
Where a man whose gods are life and breath,
Will lose his gods in the jaws of death.

[*Impressed silence.*]

PERCY: And are there – is there a part for, well, for … ?

A.P.: I should think you'd make an ideal King Darius, Percy.

PERCY: *(Beaming audibly.)* Ah! Well, that seems – yes!

MRS T.: I think if we don't get some blinkin' food soon, we ought to vote in a new chest-of-drawers to get things movin'!

A.P.: Good idea! I'd quite happily give way to a new chest-of-drawers. Right! We've got a play. I'll sort out who's playing what and allocate the other jobs like prompter and so on, then we'll have another meeting. Okay, everyone?

[*Murmurs of hungry acquiescence.*]

THYNN: Here, it's a good job we're finishing now.

A.P.: Why?

THYNN: Because I've almost run out of …

[*Click! as tape runs out.*]

TWO

SMOKE GETS IN OUR EYES

That first meeting left me a bit shell-shocked, as you can imagine, but when I got home later and had a proper look at Frank's play I felt quite encouraged. It was just right. Anne and Gerald went off to bed saying silly things like 'Goodnight Mr De Mille', and I stayed up to work out the cast list for 'Daniel in the Den'. Earlier, during the meal, I'd promised Andromeda that I'd give serious consideration to her suggestion that the play should become a modern parable, entitled: 'Daniella in the Working Men's Club', but – well, I ask you! Anyway, after a lot of thought, this was the list I finally came up with.

Narrator – Gerald Plass
Daniel – Edwin Burlesford
King Darius – Percy Brain
Servant – Elsie Burlesford
First lion – Charles Cook
Second lion – Vernon Rawlings
Third lion – Stenneth Flushpool
An angel – Victoria Flushpool
Director – Adrian Plass
Treasurer – Richard Cook
Prompter – Leonard Thynn
Costumes – Mrs Thynn & Norma Twill
Technical effects – William Farmer
Make-up – Gloria Marsh

Andromeda was not available on the date of performance, for which I sent up a brief but profoundly sincere prayer of thanks. I'm very fond of Andromeda but she is a very powerful presence when you're trying to *do* things.

As for Stenneth being a lion, well, I know he didn't put up much of a show when he read Elsie's lion poem, but I sensed how much he wanted to be in it, and besides, it occurred to me that the bit where Victoria, as an angel, had to get the lions to shut their mouths would have a very natural feel about it – in Stenneth's case anyway.

The following day I rang young William Farmer to check that he was happy to be responsible for technical effects. Happy wasn't the word! He started raving on incomprehensibly about smoke machines and coloured gels and mirror balls, whatever they might be. I just agreed with everything he said, and promised to send him a script and let him know when the next meeting was.

Surprisingly enough it was Anne who suggested I should ask Gloria Marsh to do the make-up. She said that Gloria needed to be involved and would be very useful because she'd done professional make-up once. I find Anne's attitude to Gloria oddly inconsistent. She seems to have a particular insight about which of Gloria's quite frequent requests for assistance I should respond to positively. At other times she will actually insist that we help with things I hadn't even noticed. Once, quite inexplicably, Anne and Gerald collapsed in helpless laughter after I came away from the phone to say that Gloria was asking for help in lifting a very large chest. Most odd ...

However, I digress. I did visit Gloria on the evening following that first meeting, and she was very pleased to be asked to help. She sat me down in front of a mirror and demonstrated on my face the kind of make-up she would use. It seemed to me rather bright and garish, but Gloria said it would look quite different under stage lights. We had a very pleasant coffee together after that. She really is a sweetly ingenuous person. As I left she squeezed my hand just as a child might do with her daddy, and asked if I'd forgiven her for being a naughty girl when she borrowed our car last year and bashed it.* Naturally, as a Christian,

---

*See: *The Sacred Diaries of Adrian Plass*

I forgave her wholeheartedly and agreed to her request to borrow it again next week. As I walked into the Coach and Horses on my way home I felt an unusual lightness of spirit as a result of this encounter. As Ted, the barman, pulled my usual half-pint of bitter, I said whimsically, 'I feel different, Ted.' He stared at me for a few moments then said, 'Come out the closet, 'ave yer?' It was then that I realised with alarm that I was still wearing my make-up. Needless to say, when I arrived home *very* shortly after that, Anne and Gerald and Leonard Thynn nearly died laughing when I told them what had happened.

Anyway, I'd got my list sorted out, and that was the important thing. The next morning I photocopied the script and the list on a machine at work, and sent off copies to all the people involved. I also added a note to say that there'd be a meeting of the non-acting participants on the following Monday evening, and that's what the next tape is mainly about. It doesn't start with that meeting, though. You see, every Monday evening at about half past six, Leonard gets dragged along by his mother to a rather obscure religious group called The Ninth Day Specific Bulmerites – Baroness of Wertley's Involvement. On this particular evening Leonard had his tape-recorder with him ready to come on to the 'Daniel' meeting afterwards, and he must have pressed the record button by accident, just as the 'message' started. I wasn't going to transcribe it, but Gerald said he thought it was too wonderful to leave out ...

[*Tape opens with the same crackles and hisses as the last one, followed by the typical coughs, shuffles and mutterings of a waiting congregation.*]

PREACHER: (*In a flat, monotonous, rather burdened voice.*) There are so many lessons to be learned in a garden.

CONGREGATION: (*Equally flatly.*) Ah, yes, in the garden. Amen, yes we witness to that etc.

P.: Only the other day I was trimming the privet that separates our garden from the next, and chatting uncommittedly to a non-Christian neighbour, when my ladder collapsed ...

CONG.: (*Sympathetically.*) Amen, brother ...

THYNN: Ha, ha! I mean – amen, brother.

P.: As I lay writhing on the rockery I realised, with a little spasm, that I was being taught a very important lesson. Namely, that we must expect to lose support if we start hedging.

CONG.: Amen! Thank you, Lord! Yes! etc.

P.: Recognising the providential nature of this revelation, I fetched a wooden box from the garage and, having once more ascended, re-engaged Mr Studeley in conversation. This time I was much more direct. 'Mr Studeley,' I announced, firmly, 'we are all suffering as a result of the Fall.'

CONG.: Amen! Yes! Ah! etc.

P.: '*I'm* not,' replied Mr Studeley, 'but you're bleedin' in three places.' I was about to correct his interpretation of my statement when, unfortunately, the box on which I was standing gave way with a loud crack like a pistol shot and I must have disappeared from Mr Studeley's view with quite startling suddenness.

THYNN: Hallelujah! Praise the Lord! *(Frowning silence.)* I mean – Amen, brother ...

P.: Honesty compels me to admit that as I fell backwards onto the rockery once again, I very nearly succumbed to a recurrent temptation to ascribe randomness to the events of my life. However, seeing Mr Studeley's face appear above the privet hedge at this point, I realised that here was an ideal opportunity to show joy in adversity. Abandoning my heretical impulses ...

CONG.: Praise God! Yes!

P.: ... and baring my teeth in a joyful smile, I sang the following words whilst attempting to convey that I was spreadeagled in a divinely ordained sort of way. *(Sings in a flat, joyless manner.)*

> I'm H – A – P – P – Y
> I'm H – A – P – P – Y
> I know I am
> I'm sure I am
> I'm H – A – P – P – Y

Mr Studeley said, 'Banged yer 'ead, did yer? Must 'ave!' As he withdrew, I turned my eyes away from the privet hedge, and there, less than one inch from my face, was further justification for my descent. It was only a humble slug, but – and this was the point – behind it lay a shining trail. What a graphic picture of the Christian life!

CONG.: Amen! Hallelujah! We want to be slugs for you! etc.

P.: A little later, as my wife cleaned and bandaged my wounds, I said to her, 'Wife, you are a slug among women!' She stopped bandaging and said, 'In what way, pray, do I resemble a slug?' 'It is the slime!' I cried affirmingly, 'It shines!'

CONG.: Amen! Let it shine! Let the slime shine! etc.

MRS THYNN: *(Very loudly.)* As 'e started yet?

THYNN: *(Very loud whisper.)* Turn your hearing-aid to 'T', mother, you've missed half of it!

MRS T.: Oh, good, there's only 'alf to go then.

P.: My wife is a trained nurse, so I trust there was some excellent reason why she tied my left wrist to my right ankle, and my right wrist to my left ankle before leaving rather abruptly. Bent double, I hobbled out into the garden again with little shuffling steps, and balanced carefully at the edge of the lawn to await further revelations. Mr Studeley's face appeared over the hedge again. He said, 'I was just wonderin' if you was feelin' – why are you touchin' your toes? 'Ere! Your arms an' legs is all tied together! 'Oo did that then?' Suddenly inspired, I replied, 'I am in the strings of healing, whereas you are bonded to your iniquities.'

'Too right!' said Mr Studeley, 'specially first thing in the mornin' when I get out of me bed an' try to stand up. Bonded to me iniquities, I am. Couldn't 'ave put it better meself!'

MRS T.: *(Very loudly.)* 'As 'e finished yet?

THYNN: *(Loud whisper.)* I'm not sure!

P.: I was unable to resist a slight feeling of depression as Mr Studeley disappeared again; particularly as a large apple fell heavily on the back of my head at that instant. A moment's reflection, however, showed that once again a heavenly message had been vouchsafed to me. I smiled in grateful comprehension as a larger and even heavier apple hit my head, and I toppled slowly over sideways into the rockery. I knew without doubt that my efforts with Mr Studeley would be crowned with much fruit. Amen.

CONG.: *(Frenzied response.)* Hallelujah! Amen! Oh, yes! Let there be much fruit! He toppled, he toppled! Crown his efforts! Amen! etc.

P.: We now sing number seven hundred and fifty-two in the *Ninth Day Specific Bulmerites – Baroness of Wertley's Involvement Songbook;* 'Let us rush around with ...

[*Tape clicks off*]

(Not only did Thynn not realise he'd turned his machine on and off during his hour with the Bulmerites, but when he came on to the Daniel meeting he forgot to take the pause button off until we were several minutes into the proceedings. That's why it starts in the middle of me shouting at Mrs Thynn. Also present were Leonard, Richard Cook, William Farmer, Gloria Marsh and Norma Twill, who had agreed to supervise costumes. Norma is a very pretty, single girl in her mid-twenties, who works in a factory making those pink and white marshmallows, not that it matters where she works, or that she's pretty, of course. I just mention it for information ...)

[*Tape begins abruptly as Thynn realises he's forgotten to switch on.*]

A.P.: *(Shouting.)* I did not say 'I rely on sin', I said 'hire a lion skin'! Why on earth would I say that I rely on sin, for goodness sake? All we want you to do is go along to the theatrical costumiers and hire three lion outfits! Three lion outfits! That's all!

MRS T.: I think gorillas is more frightenin'. I 'ad a dream once where this big 'airy ...

A.P.: Lions, Mrs Thynn! It's got to be lions!

MRS T.: Oh, well, you're the Bureau, you know best I s'pose.

RICHARD: Cheap!

MRS T.: Eh?

224

RICHARD: Cheap! Cheap!

MRS T.: Why's 'e doin' canary impressions?

THYNN: He's not, mother! He's saying the costumes can't be too expensive!

A.P.: We're not quite as badly off as we were, because Edwin has redirected some church funds towards this project. We haven't got money to chuck about, but we should be all right if we're careful. *(To* MRS T.*)* All we want you to do, Mrs Thynn, is make sure those three costumes are ordered and ready to be collected when the time comes! All right?!

MRS T.: All right, I'm not deaf!

NORMA: And you want the others in black tops and tights or trousers, Adrian, is that right?

A.P.: That's absolutely right, Norma. That's exactly it, and thank you for being here and taking such an invaluable part in the proceedings. Yes, black tops and tights or trousers. After all, we want to be original, don't we? Your own clothes are, if I may say so, Norma, extremely original and attractive, just as you are yourself.

NORMA: *(Blushing audibly.)* Err ... thank you. Do the black things have to have any special feature, or ... ?

RICHARD: Cheap!

MRS T.: Oh, give 'im some birdseed, someone!

A.P.: The answer to your very intelligent question, Norma, is that, beyond the fact that we can't afford to be too extravagant as Richard points out, the black clothes can be plain and simple and err ... plain. Is that okay? I do want you to feel absolutely relaxed and happy about the responsibilities that you've so kindly agreed to undertake for us. Thank you again for – well, for just being here with us. Is your chair quite comfortable? Perhaps mine would be ...

NORMA: No, I'm fine, thanks – really.

A.P.: Well, if it gets uncomfortable, just let me know and we'll exchange seats.

THYNN: My seat's not comfortable. Let's swop ...

A.P.: Be quiet, Leonard, we've got a lot to get through. Don't make a fuss. Now ...

GLORIA: I'm really looking forward to seeing Mr Brain in black tights.

[*Pause as everyone mentally envisages Percy Brain in black tights.*]

A.P.: Mmmm! Perhaps you'd better jot down 'trousers' next to Percy's name, Norma, after all ...

THYNN: We don't want to scare people off before they even see the lions, do we?

A.P.: After all, trousers look just as nice as err ... tights. Now ...

GLORIA: As for the prospect of seeing Victoria Flushpool in an angelic body-stocking, well, my cup runneth over.

THYNN: So will the body-stocking.

A.P.: Be quiet, Leonard. Err ... Norma, perhaps you'd better organise a slightly err ... fuller garment for Mrs Flushpool. I'm so sorry to mess you about. Thank you for being so patient and ...

GLORIA: I'd *love* to see *you* in tights, Adrian! Wouldn't you, Norma?

NORMA: Well, I don't – I mean, of course it would be – I mean ...

GLORIA: He's got the figure for it, hasn't he? You have you know, Adrian. Oh, I say, I haven't said something naughty, have I? You will forgive your little Gloria if she's said anything to offend you, won't you? *(Puts on a little-girl voice.)* Big smacks for naughty-warty Glorbags if daddy's cwoss wiv her!

A.P.: *(Overcoming paralysis.)* Err ... Daddy's not cwoss wiv – I mean, I'm not cross with you, Gloria. Err ... could we talk about make-up?

GLORIA: Oh, yes, of course. *(Suddenly business-like.)* Well, I don't think Gerald and Edwin and Elsie and Mr Brain will need more than basic stage make-up, so that's no problem. I've got a bit myself, but I suppose we can buy more if we need it?

A.P.: Oh, yes, as long as it's ...

226

RICHARD: Cheap! Cheap!

MRS. T.: D'you know, I reckon if we spent enough time, we could teach 'im to talk.

GLORIA: And the lions obviously won't need anything, so that brings us to the only real problem.

A.P.: Which is ... ?

GLORIA: How do we make Victoria Flushpool look like an angel?

WILLIAM: Why did you cast her in that part, Mr Plass?

A.P.: *(Miserably.)* It was a choice between telling her she wasn't in it, telling her she was playing a lion, telling her she was playing a man's part, or letting her be the angel. *(Manfully honest.)* I'm afraid ... *(Sigh.)* ... I chickened out.

THYNN: *(In sympathetic tones.)* You took the lily-livered, yellow-bellied path of abject, cowardly, pathetic refusal to face the clear path of duty. Well, who are we to judge?

A.P.: *(Coldly.)* Thank you, Leonard.

THYNN: Yes, it's good to know that a Christian brother is able to openly confess that he's a wretched, snivelling, fainthearted worm of a ...

A.P.: All right, Leonard, that'll do – thank you very much. Can we get back to the point? How do we make Mrs Flushpool into an angel? Was that the question?

THYNN: Job for Wimpey's if you ask me.

A.P.: We don't ask ...

NORMA: *(Quite stern.)* That's very unkind, if you don't mind me saying so, Mr Thynn. In fact it's very unkind even if you *do* mind me saying so. The way to make Mrs Flushpool into an angel is not just to do with clothes and make-up; it's to do with loving and caring and saying nice things, and not always trying to placate her and shut her out by making fed-up faces about her behind her back. When was the last time any of us went round to see Mrs Flushpool when we didn't actually have to? How many of us really know what goes on inside her head; what hurts her and frightens her and excites her and makes her unhappy? She's a very difficult woman. I know that. Of course I do. But I also know that Jesus never made anyone angelic by ignoring them unless he had no choice, or by saying rotten things about them when they weren't there, and neither will we!

[*A long, stunned silence.*]

A.P.: Well ...

NORMA: *(Very embarrassed.)* I – I'm sorry, I shouldn't have said all that. I had no right ...

A.P.: *(Quietly.)* I'm very glad you said it, Norma.

THYNN: Mmm ... wish I hadn't said that about err ... thingy

WILLIAM: Yeah! Well said, Norms!

GLORIA: A spot of number two, you think, Norma?

A.P.: Make-up, you mean?

NORMA: *(Softly.)* I think Gloria's talking about the command-ments, Adrian.

A.P.: Ah!

RICHARD: Certainly, some of our responses to Victoria have been somewhat ... cheap.

MRS T.: I'm goin' to give you a little bell an' a ladder for Christ-mas, Richard. *(Pause.)* Prap's we ought to be a bit nicer to the old frump – try anyway ...

[*Short silence.*]

A.P.: Perhaps we could move on to you, Leonard.

THYNN: *(Fiddling with his machine.)* Eh? Oh, yes! Me. I'm the prompter, you know.

A.P.: You're sure you can handle recording and prompting at the same time?

THYNN: *(Considers for a moment.)* Yes! Yep! No problem there.

A.P.: And you still want to do it?

THYNN: *(As though slightly hurt.)* Of course I want to do it! I *am* the prompter.

A.P.: So you're quite confident?

THYNN: Yep!

A.P.: No problems?

THYNN: No, none!

A.P.: Good! Great!

THYNN: Just one little thing ...

A.P.: Yes?

THYNN: What does a prompter do?

A.P.: *(Seething.)* He lies on the floor while the director jumps up and down on his head, Leonard. Do you honestly have no idea at all what a prompter does?

THYNN: *(Vaguely.)* I thought it was a sort of soldier.

A.P.: Why on earth ... ?

THYNN: Well, when I was about seven and at big boys' school ...

A.P.: Big boys' school, yes ...

THYNN: I went along to the first rehearsal of this school play that Miss Glanthorpe was doing ...

A.P.: Miss Glanthorpe, yes ...

THYNN: I *loved* Miss Glanthorpe!

A.P.: Get on, Leonard!

THYNN: Well, I was a bit late getting there because I had to visit the boys' tiddler room on the way – that's what we used to call it, you see.

A.P.: Really! How interesting ...

GLORIA: So sweet!

THYNN: Anyway, when I got to Miss Glanthorpe's classroom, she said, 'Ah, Lenny, you *must* be a little prompter if you want to take part in my play,' then she gave me a soldier's uniform to put on, so I thought ...

NORMA: You thought it meant a soldier?

THYNN: Yes. Doesn't it?

NORMA: *(A little weepy.)* I think that's a lovely story. I can just picture little Lenny trotting along to be in the play and getting all excited when he was given his soldier's uniform to wear. Oh, Leonard ...

GLORIA: And thinking a prompter was a soldier. Sweet!

WILLIAM: *(Shouting.)* So did you go and see Leonard playing a soldier in the school play, Mrs Thynn?!

229

MRS T.: Eh? Oh, yes, I went all right! 'E was the best one in it. Better than Hoity-toity Vera Ashby-Jones' youngest, Alfred. 'E threw up just as is mother clicked 'er camera. Lovely picture that must 'ave been. He-he!

THYNN: What is a prompter, then, if it's not a soldier?

A.P.: A prompter, Leonard, is someone who sits at the side of the stage with the script in front of him, ready to help people when they forget their lines.

THYNN: *(Mentally digesting.)* I see.... But, in that case, if Miss Glanthorpe wanted me to be a prompter and help people with their lines ...

A.P.: Yes ... ?

THYNN: Why did she dress me up as a soldier?

A.P.: No, you don't understand. When she said she wanted you to be a little prompter she meant – look, I'll explain afterwards, all right? Just as long as you understand what you've got to do in the play. *Do* you understand?

THYNN: I sit at the side of the stage ...

A.P.: On the left ...

THYNN: I sit at the side of the stage on the left, and I've got the script in front of me, and when people forget their lines, I help them ...

A.P.: By calling out clearly the first few words of the next line.

THYNN: ... by calling out clearly the first few words of the next line.

A.P.: *(Relieved.)* Good! You've got it!

THYNN: Yep!

A.P.: Good. Now, Richard, let's ...

THYNN: Just one thing ...

A.P.: Yes?

THYNN: When do I get my uniform?

A.P.: *(Wildly.)* I've just explained! You don't ...

NORMA: *(Kindly.)* Leonard, dear, you don't need a uniform to be a prompter – just ordinary clothes, that's all.

THYNN: *(Sounding terribly disappointed.)* I was looking forward to the uniform. I like uniforms. I haven't worn a uniform for nearly ...

NORMA: Adrian, couldn't Leonard wear a soldier's uniform? I'm sure I could get one quite cheaply and it doesn't really matter, does it? I mean, it doesn't, does it?

A.P.: Of course, Norma, I respect your judgment tremendously but it's not ...

GLORIA: *(Wheedlingly.)* Daddy let Lenny be a big soldier just to please his little Glorbags?

WILLIAM: Go on, Mr Plass! Say Leonard can have a uniform. Go on!

A.P.: *(In a hair-clutching sort of voice.)* I find it very difficult to believe that we are sitting here discussing what kind of costume the *prompter* should wear!

THYNN: *(Miles away.)* I *loved* Miss Glanthorpe ...

[*Silence as several pairs of reproachful eyes bore into* A.P.]

A.P.: *(A broken man.)* All right, Leonard can wear a soldier's uniform. Why not? Why should we be rational?

[*General noises of approval and satisfaction*]

GLORIA: *(Whispering.)* Big kiss for daddy afterwards for being such a huge big kind jelly-baby!

A.P.: *(Alarmed.)* Err ... that won't be necessary, Gloria, thank you very much. Now, if we could turn to finance just for a moment. As you know, Richard has kindly agreed to act as our treasurer for the duration of this project, using funds placed in the newly established Entertainment Budget. Richard has opened a special account at one of the local banks for this purpose, and I believe they've now sent you a cheque book, Richard, is that correct?

RICHARD: The bank in question has indeed now furnished me with a cheque book appropriate to the account in question, and I am therefore in a position to make withdrawals from the said account as and when the demand arises, and according to the way in which the Lord shall vouchsafe knowledge of his guiding will.

MRS T.: Eh?

THYNN: He says the boodle's on tap, mother.

RICHARD: On the contrary, Leonard. The 'boodle' is not 'on tap'. We have, after recent additions, the sum of seventy-five pounds in the aforesaid account, and I am entrusted with the stewardship of that sum. Last night, in a dream, I believe that I received a warning regarding the dangers of unworthy expenditure. I would like to share it with you now.

A.P.: Must it be now? We haven't really ...

RICHARD: *(In prophetic tones.)* I saw, as it were, an mighty herd of aardvarks flying in formation through the sky. And, behold, an voice spake unto men saying, 'Touch not these aardvarks, beyond that which shall be needful to thee for thine own sustenance, for these are mine own aardvarks set aside for mine own use.' And as I watched and marvelled, some men did

232

with mauve bows and arrows fire at and fetch down sundry aardvarks for their own sustenance and that of their kinfolk, but a goodly multitude remained and, behold, there was in this no condemnation. Then, one standing by said, 'Wherefore should we touch not these aardvarks beyond that which shall be needful for our own sustenance? Behold there existeth quite a market in aardvark skins, not to mention the attractive little knick-knacks you can make out of their teeth and so on.' And this one did then fire his arrows in mighty numbers until it did seem to rain aardvarks, and great was the falling down thereof, until they did lie as an mighty blanket upon the land, and no aardvarks flew as in the latter times. And the same voice spake saying, 'Where are mine aardvarks, set aside for mine own use? Wert thou not content to take only those aardvarks needful to thee for thine own sustenance? Wherefore hast thou taken those aardvarks which were mine own aardvarks, set aside for mine own use?' Then he that spake did wax exceeding wrath, and did cause a plague of green jerbils to afflict he who had sinned. I then awoke after a short further dream about getting into a bath full of Smarties wearing a Batman costume.

[*Stunned silence, during which you can sense* A.P. *thanking his lucky stars that Gerald's not here.*]

A.P.: Well ... I'm sure we shall all take to heart that warning not to waste a single aardvark – I mean, a single pound. Thank you, Richard. Our watchword shall be ...

RICHARD: Cheap! Cheap!

MRS T.: 'Oo's a pretty boy, then?

A.P.: Okay! All requests for expenditure should come to me first, then, if I approve it, you go to Richard for the cash. Any problems? No? Good! William, you've been sitting there patiently since we started. Let's come to you now. Edwin's taking responsibility for general stage-management, props and all that sort of thing, so basically you're in charge of sound and any special effects that you can dream up.

WILLIAM: Great! Err ... you didn't mention lights. What about the floods and the spots and the gels and the mirror-ball and the strobe and the fresnels and the follow-spots and the baby spots …

A.P.: I'm sorry, William, but apparently there's a sort of phantom of the opera type down at the hall, who crouches over the lighting board all day – and all night for all I know – and does a sort of Incredible Hulk act if anyone else even mentions touching it. We can send him a script and some suggestions, but that's about it. So it's just sound and effects, I'm afraid.

WILLIAM: That's a shame. Elsie and I have just read a book about a man in South-east Asia who saw two thousand people converted every week just through the lighting arrangement in his theatre and we thought …

A.P.: *Just* sound and effects, William …

WILLIAM: Ah, well, never mind, I could make up a really good soundtrack with stuff like thunder and roaring, and we could do some effects like smoke, and people sort of glowing and – and things.

A.P.: Exactly! Now, I think the best way to go about this is if I read the whole thing through, and you can talk about any ideas you've had as we go along. Is that okay, William?

WILLIAM: Great! Great!

A.P.: Right. Well, it starts with King Darius coming to the front of stage and addressing the audience. Here goes:

Darius: Though ruling, ruled by men with …

WILLIAM: I see smoke here! Thick, curling gouts of smoke almost obscuring the figure of the king!

A.P.: Err … right, I'll make a note of that. I'll start again, shall I? I didn't get all that err … far, did I? Right, here goes again –

Darius: Though ruling, ruled by men with hooded faces,
    Jealous, not for me, but for their honoured places.
    Lions indeed, made vicious not by hunger's pain,
    But by their lust for power and selfish gain.
    No darker hour than when I lightly penned,
    This blind agreement to destroy my servant-friend.
    Within the veil of vanity my foolish eyes,
    Perceived my greatness, but could not perceive their lies.

234

Oh, God of Daniel, guard your son tonight,
Do not defend the law, defend the right.
No sleep for me, no calm, no peace, no rest,
For I have sanctified the worst, and sacrificed the best.

Then Gerald comes on, and Darius moves over to the side looking all tragic and preoccupied, and Gerald says ...

WILLIAM: I'd see this as a moment when the – the tragedy of the moment would be best underlined by thunder – and smoke! Lots of grey, mysterious smoke creeping across the floor of the stage, really err ... mysteriously!

A.P.: *(Doubtfully.) More* smoke?

WILLIAM: Oh, yes! Really effective!

A.P.: Mmmm ... Well, anyway, we can come back to that. As I said, Gerald comes to centre-stage and speaks. He's the narrator.

Narrator: Pain is sharper than remorse,
   Death more final than regret,
   Darius will mourn tonight,
   But live his life, perhaps forget.
   While Daniel faces fearful hurt,
   Beneath the dark remorseless flood,
   That flood of fear which runs before
   The tearing down of flesh and blood.

Then, Gerald gestures behind him, and the light comes up just enough – if we can get the phantom of the opera on our side, that is – to reveal three lions sort of roaming around in the half-light, just growling softly. No sign of Daniel yet. Darius turns his head and watches the lions, and Gerald does his next bit, only it's a different rhythm – more intense and a bit faster ...

Narrator: Down in ...

WILLIAM: Can I cut in a moment?

A.P.: Yes?

WILLIAM: I've just had an idea.

A.P.: What is it?

WILLIAM: Smoke!

A.P.: Smoke again?

WILLIAM: Yes, as the tension gets going, so we release evil clouds of black smoke to show the satanic influences that ...

MRS T.: I don't know why we don't just set fire to the blinkin' theatre an' 'ave done with it. Plenty of smoke then ...

GLORIA: Aaaah, don't laugh at William's idea. I think smoke is a wonderful idea, Willy, darling.

WILLIAM: *(Blushing loudly.)* Well, I just thought ...

A.P.: All right, it's all written down. Black smoke – right. Now, Gerald's next bit ...

Narrator: Down in the den on the bone-strewn floor,
    Where the lost men scream and the lions roar,
    Where a man whose gods are life and breath,
    Will lose his gods in the jaws of death.
    Where the strong alone will hold their creed,
    In the tearing grip of the lions' greed.

Darius: *(Turning towards audience.)*
    Oh, Daniel, Daniel! save me from my madness.
    Pray your God's compassion on my sadness
    Bid him send an all-forgiving rain,
    To cool the fiery furnace of my brain.

WILLIAM: A quick thought! Rain on fire equals steam, right? We could do that using ...

A.P.: Smoke?

WILLIAM: Yes! How did you know?

A.P.: Lucky guess, I suppose. Right, now the servant comes in. That's Elsie. She's only got a little bit to say, but it's just as important. She goes over to her master, Darius, and speaks to him:

Servant: I wait upon you master as you bade me wait,
    To bring intelligence of Daniel and his fate.
    Some moments past, without complaint, or sign of care.
    I saw your servant thrown into the lions' lair.

236

Darius: Save him God, he is yours!
　　Save him from the lions' jaws!

Then Darius collapses onto his knees and more or less stays there, praying, until later on, and the servant goes off to see if there's any more news. Then we see Daniel, played by Edwin, coming slowly onto the stage, and he just sort of stands there looking at the lions with his back to the audience, while Gerald says his next bit:

Narrator: Now the moment, now the test.
　　See Jehovah's servant blessed,
　　As he stands, a trusting child,
　　Before these creatures of the wild.
　　Glad to pay the highest price,
　　To make the final sacrifice.

Now, at this stage, the lions really wake up and start to look a bit menacing – prowling around in a hungry sort of way, looking at Daniel as if he might make a good square meal. Now here, William, we really could do with a lot of ...

WILLIAM: Smoke?

A.P.: Well, I was going to say – a lot of genuine lions' roars on tape. I don't think Stenneth and Vernon and Charles are going to keep their credibility if they start bleating out unconvincing roaring noises all over the place. But as well as that we could do with some really dramatic ...

WILLIAM: Smoke! Right on!

A.P.: ... some really dramatic thunder effects.

WILLIAM: Oh ...

A.P.: That'll build up the atmosphere of danger and imminent death.

WILLIAM: Look, can I just shove a token in the fruit-machine and see if it comes up grapefruits?

A.P.: Err ... yes. I suppose so ...

WILLIAM: I just wondered (*As if it hasn't been mentioned up to now*) what you thought about smoke at this point. With the roaring and the thunder, *and* a sort of angry, swirling curtain of yellowish-black smoke it would be really atmospheric, wouldn't it?

A.P.: A bit of smoke might be appropriate here, William, but we do actually want the audience to be able to see what's happening on stage, don't we?

WILLIAM: Oh, sure! Yes, of course! Smoke here, then – I'll mark it off on my script. Great!

A.P.: Now, the roaring and the thunder ...

WILLIAM: And the smoke ...

A.P.: ... and the smoke, yes; they go on for a minute or two while Daniel sinks quietly onto his knees, facing the audience this time, and he's obviously praying quite calmly while death comes at him from behind, as it were. Then the noise goes down a bit while Daniel speaks:

Daniel: Lord of exiles, friend in strife,
    In your hands I place my life.
    Yours to take and yours to give,
    Let me die, or let me live ...

A.P.: Then Daniel bows his head and waits to be ...

MRS T.: Eaten.

A.P.: Err ... eaten, yes, or whatever, but just then ...

NORMA: Ooooh, Adrian, it's quite exciting, isn't it? It makes me go all shivery, the thought of lions suddenly attacking me. Doesn't it you, Gloria?

GLORIA: Ooooh, it does!

A.P.: Anyway, just then ...

THYNN: D'you think it's true?

RICHARD: Is what true?

THYNN: Daniel and the lions and all the rest – the fiery furnace and all that. D'you think it's true?

A.P.: I wonder if we could postpone ...

RICHARD: *(Deeply shocked.)* Of course it's true, Leonard! The story of Daniel is a part of holy Scripture, the inspired word of God. Jesus himself quoted scripture and ...

WILLIAM: I've just been reading about a man from Mauritius who was converted by a semi-colon in Leviticus! Every single jit and tattle ...

THYNN: Jat and tittle, isn't it?

NORMA: I thought it was tat and jottle ...

GLORIA: I thought it was ti ...

WILLIAM: Every single little bit is there because it's supposed to be there, and that's that!

RICHARD: The authority of scripture is absolute. It is an unshake-able rock!

THYNN: So you're not allowed to even wonder if it's true or not, then?

GLORIA: Oh, ye ...

RICHARD: No!

NORMA: *(Shyly.)* I think we're allowed to wonder anything we like, really. Edwin always says ...

THYNN: *(Remembering.)* Oh, yes ...

NORMA: Edwin always says that the Bible is a letter from God to us. He says it starts 'Dear Norma – or Richard – Or Gloria', and finishes 'Love, God', and that God meant it all to be in there, whatever you think about it.

RICHARD: Mmmm ... lets a few liberals in I suppose. The Bible's the Bible, in my view!

THYNN: My cousin, Finnegan Thynn, spent a year secretly smuggling Bibles *out* of China before he told someone what he was doing and they put him straight. He was amazed at the miraculous way the guards didn't notice what he was carrying, and when ...

GLORIA: Lenny, sweetheart, I think we're telling little porky-pies, aren't we?

MRS T.: 'Course 'e is! Can't imagine a Thynn bein' that stupid! I think the Bible's a good ...

A.P.: Do forgive me for interrupting this fascinating theological discussion, but there is a little matter of a play to be attended to, and we haven't finished yet.

[*Murmured 'sorries' etc.*]

WILLIAM: Can I just ... ?

A.P.: No, William, I'd really rather you didn't. As I was saying a very long time ago, just then, just as Daniel finishes saying his bit, and the roaring and thunder ...

THYNN: And smoke!

WILLIAM: Thank you, Leonard.

THYNN: Don't mention it, William.

WILLIAM: I appreciate it.

THYNN: Really, it was ...

A.P.: The roaring and the thunder and the ...

A.P./THYNN/WILL: Smoke.

A.P.: ... increase in intensity, until a figure enters the lions' den from the side, and that's Mrs Flushpool as the angel. She moves slowly among the lions, touching each one on the head as she goes, and as she touches them they settle down and purr like cats. So the roaring and thunder die away completely

240

until everything's quiet. Then Daniel stands up, turns to the angel, and says ...

WILLIAM: The smoke stays, then?

A.P.: Sorry?

WILLIAM: You said the thunder and roaring dies away, but you didn't mention the smoke. I think it's a great idea to keep the smoke. We could have gentle, soothing, everything's-all-right sort of smoke, couldn't we? It could be ...

A.P.: *(Quietly.)* William?

WILLIAM: Yes?

A.P.: Don't be silly.

WILLIAM: Right ...

A.P.: *(Muttering to himself.)* Everything's-all-right sort of smoke! Honestly! *(Normal tones.)* Daniel stands up, turns to the angel, and says:

Daniel: Now indeed I sing your praises,
    Now indeed all terror flees,
    For I see your sovereign power,
    Even over beasts like these.

And the angel answers him:

Angel: God's own servant, fear me not,
    Love and joy and peace are yours,
    God has sent his holy angel,
    I have closed the lions' jaws.
    Here they lie, those mighty killers,
    Harmless where great harm has been,
    Sleep and when the dawn has risen,
    Tell the king what you have seen.

Then the angel wafts off, and everything goes dark – Incredible Hulk permitting – and then the lights come up, and the lions and Daniel have gone, and there's just Darius there, calling out to Daniel.

Darius: Servant of the living God, hear my anguish!
    Has he kept his hand upon you in your danger?

Does your God have power to rescue you from danger?
Daniel, speak to me!

Then Daniel appears:

Daniel: Live for ever mighty king,
God's own angel took my part,
Evil has no power to harm
People who are pure of heart.
He subdued your hungry lions,
On their heads he laid his hand,
So it is you see your servant,
Happy now before you stand.

Then the last speech is from Darius:

Darius: Such a God deserves a people,
And I vow it shall be so,
Every soul within this land,
Shall kneel and praise the God you know.

And that's it! Thunderous applause, we win the prize, and we all go home. Okay?

[Pause.]

THYNN: I really, really *loved* Miss Glanthorpe ...

GLORIA: Jot and tittle! That's it! Jot and tittle! Got it!

A.P.: *(Suspiciously.)* You have been listening to the play, haven't you?

NORMA: *(Earnestly.)* Oh, yes, Adrian, and it's really good! Mr Braddock is ever so clever. We've all enjoyed hearing it ever so much.

A.P.: Well, thank you, Norma, and I've enjoyed ...

MRS T.: 'As 'e finished readin' that mouldy old play yet?

WILLIAM: It's not a mouldy old play, Mrs Thynn. It's absolutely great! I'm going to ring up Stage Gear and book a smoke machine as soon as I get home!

A.P.: *(Hastily.)* We haven't actually agreed on exactly where we're going to have smoke, have we, William? Do bear that in mind, won't you?

WILLIAM: Of course! Don't worry, I'll make sure there's enough smoke.

A.P.: That's not quite – oh, never mind now. I'll ring you up later to talk about it. Everyone else quite clear?

[*Chorus of 'yes', 'yep', 'fine' etc.*]

MRS T.: '*Ow* many tiger skins?

A.P.: *LION* SKINS!! THREE *LION* SKINS!! OKAY?!!

MRS T.: That's what I thought – no need to get difficult, I'll gettem!

A.P.: Good! Norma? Richard? William? Gloria? Leonard? Questions? Problems? No? Right, I'll let you all know when the next meeting is. Thanks for coming.

[*Rustling of paper and noise of farewells until only* A.P. *and* THYNN *remain.* THYNN *is making a sort of snuffling noise.*]

A.P.: (*Gently.*) Leonard, what's the matter? You're not ... ?

THYNN: M – M – M – Miss G – G – G – Glanthorpe! I m – m – m – miss her!

A.P.: (*A bit out of his depth.*) But, Leonard, that was years and years ago. She must be ...

THYNN: She used to tell me I was good at things. I liked that. I'd forgotten ...

[*Long pause.*]

A.P.: Errr ... shall I pray with you, Leonard?

THYNN: To God, you mean?

A.P.: Err ... yes, to God.

THYNN: Yes, please.

A.P.: All right, well let's turn the tape off first.

THYNN: Oh, yes, I'd forgotten about ...

[*Click! as tape-recorder is turned off.*]

THREE

A GIRAFFE CALLED MR HURD

That second meeting wasn't too bad, but it left me with one or two misgivings. William clearly saw the whole thing as a sort of continuous smoke-screen, interrupted from time to time by actors peering through the fog searching for an audience to deliver lines to. I had an awful feeling that if I wasn't very firm with Master Farmer the production would be more appropriately entitled 'Daniel Gets Lost', or 'Daniel in the Smoke Den'.

My other concern was about Mrs Thynn. Her incredible capacity for getting hold of the wrong end of the stick (a capacity inherited to an almost clone-like extent by Leonard – I'd seen no reason to doubt the Finnegan Thynn story) could prove a problem, simple though her task was. Other than that, I was quite pleased. I even began to indulge in little day-dreams where people shook me by the hand after the performance and said things like, 'This is undoubtedly a major contribution to the world of Christian drama.' Then I'd say things like, 'Really, I had very little to do with it,' and they'd smile at me, rather impressed with my quiet modesty, and know that, actually, I was absolutely *central* to the whole project. It was a very pleasant, warming sort of picture. If I'd known what was really going to happen I'd have booked my passage with Gerald's friend, Gary, and gone off to do something feasible like converting Greenland. Not having the gift of foretelling the future, however, I pressed on quite optimistically.

Leonard asked me if I'd come round the next evening so that we could practise 'being a prompter' and that's where this next tape, a shorter one, was made. When I arrived, he said that he'd just recorded a prayer about the production, and would I like to hear it? This was it.

THYNN: *(Shouting.)* I'm just going to do some recording, mother!

MRS T.: *(A distant voice, probably in the kitchen.)* All accordin' to what, Leonard?

THYNN: *(Louder.)* No, mother! I said I'm about to record on tape!

MRS T.: Can't afford to escape what?

THYNN: *(Almost screaming.)* I'M RECORDING SOMETHING! PLEASE DON'T DISTURB ME!!

MRS T.: Bees don't disturb *me* either, specially when there aren't any, like there aren't 'ere. Are you goin' loony, Leonard?

THYNN: *(Actually screaming.)* I'M RECORD ... !! Hold on, I'll come through there ... *(Very faint muttering as he goes.)* It'd only be about six years with good behaviour ... *(Speaks loudly in the distance.)* Mother, I'm going to do some record-ing: Would you mind not disturbing me?

MRS T.: 'Course I don't mind. Why didn't you say so?

THYNN: *(Muttering again as he returns to the living room.)* I *did*, you deaf old – person. *(Sound of door closing.)* Right, now I can get down to prayer. Sitting or kneeling? I think I'll sit. After all, we're not supposed to make pointless rules for our-selves. *(Creak of armchair springs followed by a pause.)* On the other hand there's nothing wrong with kneeling down, and maybe it's big-headed to think I can sit, when people who're better than me are kneeling ... *(Sound of armchair creaking again as Thynn kneels down. Pause.)* I don't know though – Edwin said the other day that being comfortable's the main thing, and my legs go to sleep when I kneel for a long time. Think I'll stand. *(Pause and slight huffing and grunting noises as Thynn gets to his feet.)* This is silly! I can't relax while I'm standing up. Maybe I could kneel on the floor and put my head on the armchair – no, I'll fall asleep if I do that. P'raps if I squat on the floor with my back to the wall ...

MRS T.: *(In the distant distance.)* Adrian's goin' to be 'ere soon! 'Ave you got through yet?

THYNN: *(Creak of springs as Thynn sits in armchair.)* Sorry, God! I'd better get on with it or there'll be no time left. It err … it's me again, God. Thynn – Leonard Thynn, thirty-five Postgate Drive, just past the King's Head and second on the left as you go round the pond. I err … I hope my position's all right – not too err … relaxed or err … arrogant. I could kneel if you like, or squat, or hang over the back of my chair with my head on the floor, or anything really. I hope you don't mind me bothering you again, but I feel a bit err … funny, so I thought I would. Bother you, that is. Got a bit upset yesterday thinking about – thinking about – well, thinking about Miss Glanthorpe and when I was small and all. Got thinking about things. Me. Things in the past, God. About never doing much – being much. Got thinking about the old hooch – booze – drink – alcohol. Haven't done too badly lately, God. Almost forgotten what the inside of the old King's Head looks like. I always go the long way round to avoid Wally's off-licence. Haven't had a drink for a while. Not that I don't want one! Oh, *God* I want one! Get a bit cross with poor old mother sometimes, too. Suppose you couldn't sort her ears out – do us all a favour? No, well, up to you, of course, just a thought … Anyway, the point is, I don't want to be a – a Jonah in this Daniel thing. You remember Jonah? Sorry, silly question. 'Course you knew him – friend of yours. Your whale too, presumably. None of my business, naturally. I just don't want to mess it all up for the others by not being – not being – I don't know … good enough, or something when I'm being a soldier – prompter I mean. So, if you could sort of look after everybody who's in it, and make sure what they do doesn't get messed up by what I do, if you see what I mean, and if my uniform could be a – a good one, that would be err … good. And I'm sorry I said that about Mrs Flushpool and Wimpey's, and err … that's about it for now I think, God. Thank you for listening. Amen.

[*Click!* as recorder goes off, followed by *click!* as THYNN switches to 'RECORD' after playing his prayer to me.]

THYNN: Sounds a bit silly played back, doesn't it?

A.P.: It doesn't sound silly at all, Leonard. Better than most of my prayers. I seem to just flip tiddly-winks up most of the time. I hope I don't mess up what everybody else does as well.

MRS T.: *(From the kitchen.)* D'you want coffee, Adrian?

A.P.: *(Shouting.)* Yes please, Mrs Thynn!

MRS T.: D'you want coffee, Adrian?

A.P.: *(Bellowing.)* Yes please, Mrs Thynn!! Two sugars!!

MRS T.: D'you want coffee, Adrian?

A.P.: *(Trying to inject politeness into apoplexy.)* YES PLEASE! TWO SUGARS!

MRS T.: 'Ow many sugars?

A.P.: TWO!!

MRS T.: I'll bring the sugar through then you can 'ave what you like.

A.P.: *(Weakly.)* Thank you ...

THYNN: Right, let's get on with the prompting practice.

A.P.: Okay, Leonard. Now, let's see ... you sit over on that chair as though you were sitting at the side of the stage, and I'll stand in the middle of the room as if I was acting. Got your script?

THYNN: Yep!

A.P.: Good! I've got one too, so we're all set.

THYNN: *(Sounding very alert and business-like.)* Right!

A.P.: Now ...

THYNN: We'll just pretend I've got my uniform on, shall we?

A.P.: Err ... yes, all right, Leonard. Now, let's imagine that I'm Percy Brain playing King Darius.

THYNN: Right.

A.P.: And I've just come on stage right at the beginning of the play. I'm feeling very nervous ...

THYNN: So am I, don't worry.

A.P.: No, I don't mean *I'm* feeling very nervous. I mean I'm pretending to be Percy Brain and *he's* very nervous.

THYNN: *(Intelligently.)* Ah, right! With you ...

248

A.P.: The curtain's up and the audience is waiting for me to start. With me?

THYNN: Yep!

A.P.: So, off I go *(rustle of script)*. Ready?

THYNN: Ready!

A.P.: *(A vaguely Brain-like impression.)*
   Though ruling, ruled by men with hooded faces,
   Jealous, not for me, but for their honoured places.
   Lions indeed, made ... err ... made ... err ... made err ...
   (Pause.) Leonard, why aren't you telling me what the rest of the line is?

THYNN: I don't need to.

A.P.: *(Blankly.)* Why not?

THYNN: Because you've got a script. You can look for yourself.

A.P.: *(With rising hysteria.)* But that's because we're pretending! On the night Percy *won't* be holding a script – he'll have learned his lines!

THYNN: He won't need prompting in that case, will he?

A.P.: BUT IF HE'S NERVOUS, YOU ID ... !

[*A.P.'s raging interrupted by bumps and clatters as* MRS T. *enters with the coffee.*]

MRS T.: 'Ere you are, nice cuppa coffee! 'Ow's it goin'?

THYNN: Adrian says Percy Brain's going to forget his lines on the night, mother.

A.P.: No I did *not* say that! Percy Brain forgetting his lines is purely hypothetical.

MRS T.: I agree, specially at 'is age. Anyway, I'll leave you to get on with it.

[*Bumps and door-slam as* MRS T. *exits*]

A.P.: Perhaps I haven't made it quite clear, Leonard. Shall we go through it slowly again?

THYNN: *(Confidently.)* Okay!

A.P.: On the night when we do the play, Percy Brain – it could be anyone, but we're using him as an example – might get very nervous and forget his lines, even though he's actually learned them and got them in his head. Right?

THYNN: Yep!

A.P.: So you're there to help when that happens. If someone starts a line and can't remember the end of it, you're the one who reminds him or her what it is. If they can't remember how a speech starts, they'll probably say 'PROMPT', then you'll know they need help. Understand?

THYNN: Got it!

A.P.: *(Lacking faith.)* Really?

THYNN: Yep! If they forget their lines, it's up to me!

A.P.: Good! Now, let's have another go. That great big china giraffe on the wall unit's going to be the audience, right?

THYNN: Right! He's called Mister Hurd because ...

A.P.: So I come on, pretending to be Percy ...

THYNN: Pretending to be King Darius.

A.P.: Yes, and I, or rather, *he,* is very nervous.

THYNN: Right!

A.P.: Script ready?

THYNN: Script ready!

A.P.: Know what to do?

THYNN: Firing on all cylinders, Sah!

A.P.: Err ... right, here we go then:
Though ruling, ruled by men with hooded faces.
Jealous, not for me, but for their honoured places,
Lions indeed, made vicious not by hunger's pain,
But by their lust for power and selfish gain.
Err ... err ... Prompt!

[*Rustle of script and creak of chair springs as Thynn stands up and, watched with dumb disbelief by* A.P., *moves to the centre of the room and addresses the china giraffe with loony sauvity.*]

THYNN: Good evening, Mister Hurd. My name's Leonard Thynn and, as you can tell by my uniform, I'm the prompter. Now,

Percy's having trouble getting started on the fifth line, so I'm here to help him out. Percy, the line you're looking for is: 'No darker hour than when I lightly penned'. See you later Mister Hurd, whenever anyone's nervous, in fact. Remember: Thynn's the name, prompting's the game! Goodnight and God bless until we meet again!

[*Thynn returns to his chair, waving to the giraffe as he goes.* A.P. *stands, silently transfixed, for quite a long time.*]

THYNN: *(Modestly.)* I thought those extra bits up all on my own.

A.P.: *(A little, quiet, 'what's-happened-to-the-real-world?' sort of voice.)* Leonard ...

THYNN: Yes?

A.P.: The prompter doesn't come on stage, Leonard. He stays out of sight, Leonard. He doesn't say 'Thynn's the name, prompting's the game,' Leonard. He doesn't say anything except little bits of lines to help the person who *is* on stage, Leonard. Are you sure you ought to be the prompter, Leonard?

THYNN: Well, I did it all right when I was in Miss Glanthorpe's play. *(Hastily.)* I know that was different, but – but I do want to be the prompter, I really do ... I think I've got it now. I sit at the side of the stage, out of sight, and when people forget their lines I help them by calling out the next bit. How's that. *Let* me be ...

A.P.: All right, Leonard. Okay, okay, okay, okay, okay! One more chance. Okay?

THYNN: Yep! Okay!

A.P.: Right. I'll use a different bit of the script, the bit that starts 'Down in the den ...' – the narrator's bit. Got it?

THYNN: *(Frantic rustling of scripts.)* Err ... got it!

A.P.: You sit on that chair. *Stay* on that chair!

THYNN: Fine – no problem ...

A.P.: And I'll be Gerald addressing the giraffe from over here. Okay so far?

THYNN: Ace!

A.P.: Sure?

THYNN: Ace cubed!

A.P.: Here we go then. Last chance!

THYNN: *(Humbly.)* Last chance ...

A.P.: Off we go then:
Down in the den on the bone-strewn floor,
Where the lost men scream and the lions roar,
Where a man whose gods are life and breath
Will lose his gods in the jaws of death
Where the strong alone ... err ... prompt!

THYNN: Will hold their creed ...

A.P.: Where the strong alone will hold their creed, In the tearing grip of the ... err ... err ... prompt!

THYNN: Lions' greed!

A.P.: In the tearing grip of the lions' greed ... That's it, Leonard! You've done it! You've got it right!

THYNN: *(Clearly astounded.)* I have?

A.P.: That was perfect. Well done!

THYNN: So I *am* the prompter?

A.P.: You certainly are, Leonard.

THYNN: I really understand now, don't I?

A.P.: You really do! Well, I must fly, Leonard. I'll see you later. Thank your mother for the coffee. I haven't got much voice left. Bye!

THYNN: Yes, 'bye then! See you later ... *(sound of doors opening and closing as* A.P. *leaves. After a few moments Thynn's voice can be heard in the kitchen as he speaks to his mother.)* Adrian said thank you for the coffee, mother!

MRS T.: 'E's welcome. 'Ow'd you get on with your wha'snamin'?

THYNN: Brilliant! I really understand it now. By the way, I hope you don't mind, but Adrian wants to borrow your big china giraffe for the evening of the performance. It's going to be the audience.

MRS T.: You'll 'ave to speak up, darlin'. I'm gettin' a bit deaf in me old age. I thought for a minute you said my big china giraffe was goin' to be the audience on the night of the play.

THYNN: I did say that, mother. It's the only bit I don't really understand. I've got to stay right out of sight in my soldier's uniform so that the giraffe can't see me when Percy Brain forgets his lines.

MRS T.: *(Suspiciously.)* You 'aven't bin back on the bottle again, 'ave you, Leonard?

THYNN: 'Course not, mother! I'm just telling you what Adrian told me. Apart from that, I understand everything perfectly ...

MRS T.: That's nice, Leonard ... 'Ave you switched your thing off?

[*Click! as Thynn rushes in to switch his machine off.*]

FOUR

DIRECTING *GANDHI* WOULD BE SIMPLER ...

It wasn't until long after the performance of 'Daniel', that I heard the end of that third tape and realised why Thynn was so puzzled when he saw real people arriving to watch the performances at the drama festival. It also explained why he brought his three-foot-high china giraffe along and sat it in the middle of the front row. As soon as the seats started to fill up, his mighty brain must have realised the truth, because he went out and retrieved it. He stood it outside the men's toilet in the dressing room and said it was a mascot. The end of the tape also explains the origin of a persistent local rumour to the effect that the Home Secretary, Douglas Hurd, would be gracing the festival with his presence. I never did get round to asking the Thynns why they thought Mister Hurd was an appropriate name for a china giraffe. The way Leonard's mind works is one of the world's great unsolved mysteries. Still – he had got the hang of prompting, just about, so that was one more job done.

The next thing that happened was me getting neurotic about whether people had learned their lines or not. We only had time for two proper rehearsals before actually performing the thing, so it was essential that people had made a real stab at learning their parts. After all, no one had *that* much to say. Anne said I shouldn't phone people and check because I always end up in a bad temper; a gross exaggeration, but I thought it best to wait until she and Gerald were out. Unfortunately, they both came in with Thynn in tow just as I'd dialled Elsie's number and was waiting for someone to answer. When I told them what I was doing, Anne sighed, Gerald chuckled and Thynn whipped his ridiculous machine off his shoulder and stuck the microphone right next to the phone so that he could pick up both ends of the conversation. In some places I've put down what I *wanted* to say, in contrast with what I *did* say ...

[*Click of recorder being switched on, followed by sound of receiver being picked up at the other end.*]

A.P.: *(With forced casualness.)* Hello, who's that?

ELSIE: *(For it is she.)* You don't think I'm stupid enough to give my name to potential telephone perverts, do you?

A.P.: I'm sorry, Elsie – it's Adrian Plass here.

ELSIE: I know, I recognised your voice.

A.P.: Well, why bother with all the telephone pervert stuff, then?

ELSIE: It's the principle. I'm training men.

A.P.: Oh, I see, well, consider me trained. Look here, Elsie, I'm ringing about your lines.

ELSIE: What lines?

A.P.: *What* lines? *Your* lines – in the play!

ELSIE: What play's that?

A.P.: *(With controlled but rapidly mounting fury.)* The play, Elsie! The Daniel play! The play we sat and talked about for goodness knows how long last Monday! The play we're doing at the Drama Festival. You *must* remember!

ELSIE: Oh, am I in that? Yes, I do remember something vaguely about it. Well, you might have given me a script. It'll never be ready if you don't get the scripts out on time, will it?

A.P.: *(What I actually said, using massive self-control and Christian restraint.)* Elsie, my darling, I think you'll find, if you look, that I *have* sent you a script – some days ago, actually – and I really would be ever so grateful if you could just learn those four little lines by this Friday evening, which, as you'll see if you read the note I sent with the script, is when the first of our only two rehearsals is due to happen. So, as you can see, it really is important to get learning.

[*What I wanted to say while holding Elsie upside down over a vat of boiling oil)* You stupid egocentric, fluffy-haired twit of an adolescent! Why haven't you been eating and sleeping and breathing this play like I have, through every second of every minute of every hour of every day since I was foolish enough to start this whole horrendous exercise! And if, you empty-headed little ratbag, you haven't learned every single letter of every single word of every single line in your miserable little speech by Friday, I shall dunk you like a fancy biscuit into this boiling oil! Do I make myself clear?]

ELSIE: Well, if you say you've sent it I suppose you must have. I'll try to glance at it before Friday if I get a moment. Wait a minute! Friday, did you say? William and I go out on Fridays. That's our night! *(With heavy reluctance.)* I suppose we *could* come out to this rehearsal of yours if we absolutely had to ...

A.P.: *(What I actually said.)* I'd be so grateful if you could organise things so that it's possible to be there, Elsie.

[*What I wanted to say whilst waving a magnum pistol under her nose)* Go ahead – don't turn up! Make my week, punk!]

ELSIE: *(Sighing.)* I suppose I'll be there, then. Hold on a minute – William's here. He's saying something ... *(Pause with distant muttering.)* William says he's got the smoke machine, and he's had lots more ideas about how to use it in the play.

A.P.: Oh, good, yes, that's err ... good.

ELSIE: *(Powerfully.)* Mr Plass, I'm a Christian, so I forgive you freely for rejecting what I wrote as though it was a piece of rubbish, nor do I feel anger or resentment about your feeling that I look enough like a *boy* to be cast as a male servant! However, I would get very upset if I thought that William's creativity was being crushed.

A.P.: *(Sweetly.)* You've remembered an awful lot about the play suddenly, Elsie.

ELSIE: Yes – well ... anyway, just as long as the most important person in the whole thing doesn't get ...

A.P.: Meaning William?

ELSIE: Of course! Just as long as William doesn't get ...

A.P.: Crushed ...

ELSIE: Exactly!

A.P.: *(With superhuman control.)* I shall do my very best not to crush any aspect of William, Elsie.

ELSIE: Good! Well, I expect I'll see you on Friday, Mr Plass. I can't stay talking any longer. William's just bought a book about a man in the Solomon Islands who converted people by scratching their names on trees then laying hands on the bark. We're just going up to Hinkley Woods to do a few before suppertime. We thought we'd do it road by road until the whole town's done. It may be that there's time for us to look at the play later on this evening. We'll see.

A.P.: Thank you *very* much, Elsie. How *very* kind of you. Goodbye.

[*Sound of receiver being placed gently down, then ground viciously into its cradle.*]

ANNE: I don't know why you bother, darling. I told you you'd end up in a bad temper. Why don't you just leave them? They'll learn their lines all right. You get yourself in such a state!

A.P.: I am not in a state!

ANNE: You are, you've got those little white bits at the corners of your mouth. You're in a state!

GERALD: And you keep rubbing the back of your neck with your hand. You always do that when you're in a state.

THYNN: *(Suicidally.)* Say something into the microphone about being in a state.

[*Sound of vicious dialling.*]

ANNE: You're not ringing someone else, surely, Adrian. It'll only get worse, you know it will! Why don't you come and have a nice cup of tea and forget ...

A.P.: *(Grim.)* Hello, is that Percy? – Get that microphone out of my nose, Leonard – Percy, I'm just checking that you've learned your lines okay ...

PERCY: An actor prepares! I am engaged in all aspects of what promises to be a highly demanding role! I have been soaking myself in historical and biblical references to kingship in ancient Babylon. I dwell within the skin of King Darius!

A.P.: Have you learned your lines, Percy?

PERCY: I shall proceed according to the tenets of the master, Stanislavski. I shall build a character upon the rock of my own personality. Layer upon layer, nuance upon nuance, like some insubstantial phantom slowly gaining flesh and blood reality, the person I am to become will emerge, and live!

A.P.: Have you learned your lines, Percy?

PERCY: I have delved deep into the very entrails of the *meaning* of the words, and I am discovering ...

A.P.: Have you learned your lines, Percy?

PERCY: I am immersed in ...

A.P.: Have you learned your lines, Percy?

PERCY: I have ...

A.P.: Have you learned your lines, Percy?

PERCY: I ...

A.P.: HAVE YOU LEARNED YOUR LINES, PERCY?

PERCY: No, I have not! I must not be troubled by such trivial details at this stage in my flow through the estuary of rehearsal towards the deep ocean of performance!

A.P.: You'll end up in the little dribble of not being in it, if you don't learn your lines, Percy. Do I make myself clear?

PERCY: *(After a little rumbling.)* Possibly the optimum moment has arrived for a little vulgar line-learning. Rest assured I shall err ... attend to it. In fact, I shall err ... attend to it now. Farewell!

A.P.: *(Through his teeth.)* Farewell, Percy!

[*Sound of phone slamming down.*]

GERALD: It's wonderful how you manage to stay cool, dad. You'd make a good nun.

THYNN: You've got the feet for it.

A.P.: What do you mean, I've got the feet for it?

THYNN: Well, you know those King peng ...

ANNE: Darling, don't make any more calls – please! You'll end up marching up and down the hall blowing through your nose and muttering to yourself. Why not just leave it?

GERALD: Yeah, leave it, dad. You can trust Edwin to learn his lines, and you wouldn't have the nerve to ask Mrs Flushpool if she's learned her words, so ...

ANNE: Gerald, you really are unbelievably silly sometimes!

[*More vicious dialling.*]

A.P.: *(Hums tensely as he waits.)* Hello, is that Vic – Leonard, I shall insert that microphone into you if you don't hold it away from my face – I'm sorry, is that Vict ...

MRS F.: Who is that?

A.P.: Hello, Victoria, it's Adrian Plass here. I just phoned to ask you – *(Suddenly remembers the new 'be nice to MRS F.' decision)* to ask you err ... how you are. *(Lamely.)* How are you?

MRS F.: *(A little taken aback.)* I am well, and rejoicing in my daily defeat of the natural. Today I have eschewed chiropody. My feet were a thorn in my flesh.

A.P.: Really ... Good! Well, I also wanted to ask you err ... *(nerve gone)* how Stenneth is.

MRS F.: Stenneth is seated at the pianoforté perusing a new and most instructive book – *Sermons Set to Music,* by Doctor Martyn Lloyd Webber. He is quite content.

A.P.: Good, good! That's good ...

MRS F.: Was there something else, Adrian? I am at present ...

A.P.: There was just one thing – err ... I wondered if you've yet managed to – to ...

MRS F.: Yes?

A.P.: To err ... to plan your holiday for next year.

MRS F.: We do not take holidays, Adrian. We do not *believe* in holidays. We undertake periods of recreational outreach.

A.P.: Ah, I see ... well, where are you planning to err ... undertake your period of recreational outreach next year?

MRS F.: Benidorm.

A.P.: Ah ... yes, very commendable ...

MRS F.: If there's nothing else, I really ought to get on with ...

A.P.: *(Desperately.)* I really did just want to – to know ...

[*Sound of Gerald making chicken noises in the background.*]

MRS F.: To know what?

A.P.: To know – to know err ...

MRS F.: Adrian, I am engaged in the task of learning my lines for the forthcoming dramatic production. I should like to continue with this task if at all possible!

A.P.: Ah! Right! Fine! Good! Sorry! Of course! Yes! Goodbye! See you later ...

MRS F.: God willing, yes. Goodbye.

[*Sound of* A.P.'s *telephone being dropped onto its cradle.*]

GERALD: Have you got anything you want to melt, mum? You could use dad's face.

ANNE: Be quiet, Gerald! She was in the middle of learning them, was she, darling?

A.P.: *(After inhaling long and deeply through his nose.)* Yes. She was in the middle of learning them, Anne. If you don't stop following me around with that infernal mechanical lollipop, Leonard, you'll be recording your own death rattle.

ANNE: Anyway, you've checked everyone now, darling, except Edwin, and Gerald's quite right in saying that you can trust Edwin. Don't you think so?

A.P.: *(Sounds of weary chair-sinking.)* Oh, yes, I'm sure Edwin will do his stuff. I dunno ... it's hard work, this directing business.

GERALD: It's good practice for saying: 'Do I make myself clear', though, dad. You must've said that at least, ooh, let me see ...

A.P.: Thank you so much for your chicken imitation while I was on the phone, Gerald. It was most helpful and encouraging. Now, if you don't mind I'm going to – wait a minute!

ANNE: *(Quite alarmed.)* What is it, Adrian? Why are you looking at Gerald like that?

A.P.: *(In slow, menacing tones.)* There's just one other person we haven't checked. Isn't there, Gerald?

GERALD: Is there, dad?

A.P.: Yes, Gerald. You! I forgot all about you. You've got about twenty lines to learn, haven't you?

GERALD: Err ... yes, that's about right ...

A.P.: So how are we doing, my little chicken imitator? How many of our lines have we learned since we got our script? Eh?

GERALD: *(Airily.)* Oh, I don't think it matters if you don't learn a script word for word. As long as you get the general sense, that's all that really counts. I'll just fudge along and more or less busk it. The rhymes don't add that much to it after all, do they?

[Short pre-eruptive silence.]

ANNE: *(Aghast.)* Gerald! What ... ?

A.P.: *(A murderously incredulous growl.)* Fudge along ... ? More or less busk it ... ? Rhymes don't add that much to it ... ? I'll teach you whether it matters if you don't learn a script word for word!

[Sound of banging and crashing as A.P. chases Gerald around the room.]

262

GERALD: *(Sounding, appropriately, like someone undergoing the pain of a half-nelson.)* Only joking, dad! Only joking! Listen:

> Pain is sharper than remorse,
> Death more final than regret,
> Darius will mourn tonight,
> But live his life, perhaps forget.
> While Daniel faces fearful hurt,
> Beneath the dark remorseless flood.
> That flood of fear which runs before
> The tearing down of flesh and blood.

I know all the rest as well! Really I do! Listen:

Down in the den on the ...

A.P.: You know it? You've learned it? You've ...

GERALD: Of course. Got it off pat more or less immediately.

A.P.: So you thought you'd just give my blood pressure a little exercise, did you? Thanks a lot!

[*Sound of door opening and slamming as* A.P. *stomps off into the hall.*]

ANNE: Honestly, Gerald. When will you learn?

GERALD: Sorry, mum. Just couldn't resist it *(Chuckles.)* Went up like a volcano, didn't he?

THYNN: What's he doing now?

ANNE: He'll be doing just what I said he'd end up doing – marching up and down the hall blowing through his nose and muttering to himself.

THYNN: *(Excitedly.)* I must get that on tape!

ANNE: I really wouldn't ...

[*Door opens and slams shut as* THYNN *disappears into the hall. Muffled sounds of conflict end with a muffled cry, and abrupt silence as the recorder is either deliberately or accidentally switched off.*]

FIVE

AN ANGEL UNAWARE

I didn't kill Thynn in the hall. I quenched him with a very heavy old army greatcoat which happened to switch his machine off at the same time. I must admit I was a little miffed. I was beginning to feel a bit ashamed of the whole exercise really, if I'm honest. I hadn't lost my temper so much or so badly for a long time, and it wasn't exactly bringing out the best in others either. The day after not killing Thynn I decided to pop round and see Bill Dove. Bill and Kitty Dove had been my favourite elderly couple for years. They were amazingly good at making things seem 'okay' again – especially Kitty. When she died nearly a year ago, I was very upset. Anne and I tried to get round to see Bill every week or so.

'The thing is, Bill,' I said, 'that we don't get all this conflict – or hardly any of it – in services or church meetings. People make an effort to get on with each other, and things go more or less smoothly. Perhaps it's a big mistake to do this sort of thing.'

Bill chuckled like he always does. 'That's the 'ole point, mate! 'Seasy ter be all lovey-dovey in church an' that, innit? Piece o' cake! Summink like this what your doin', well, ain't so easy to keep the old pretendin' up, is it? Little bit of aggro – little bit of sortin' out – do us all good. Find out what's 'appenin' behind the old crinkly smiles, eh?'

'I don't think there's much happening behind my crinkly smile, Bill,' I said dismally. 'I seem to spend all my time getting irritable and telling people off.'

'Yer know what Kitty'd say if she was 'ere now, doncher, mate?'

'What would she say, Bill?'

'First of all she'd say 'ave another doughnut, Adrian. Then she'd say 'ow good it was that you was takin' on somethin' like this for Jesus, an 'ow if 'e wants you to do it, 'e'll make sure it ends up right. But ...'

He leaned forward and tapped me on the chest. "is idea of endin' up right might not be the same as your idea of endin' up right! An' it 'asn't got to matter! With me?'

'Yes, Bill,' I said. 'I think I'm with you – I do miss Kitty sometimes, Bill.'

'So do I, mate,' said Bill, smiling and sighing, 'so do I ...'

The first of our two rehearsals was planned for the following Friday. We booked Unity Hall specially for the purpose, and I arranged that the actors should come early, so that we could do some rather interesting warm-up exercises from a book I'd bought called *The Third Book of Theatrical Themes for Theological Thespians*. Nearly everybody was there on time. Gerald, Percy, Edwin, Charles, Vernon and Stenneth were all there by five past seven. Stenneth explained that Victoria would be a little late as she was in the middle of speaking to a neighbour about his son's musical excesses, but would get there as soon as she could. Thynn was there early as well, thinking he'd be allowed to sit on the side and laugh at us. I said he could only stay if he left his machine switched on and joined in properly. There was no sign of Elsie by the time we got started. Just before we began I reminded everybody – including Stenneth, who seemed terribly pleased – that we were going to make an extra special effort to be nice to Victoria starting from when she first walked through the door this evening. Everyone nodded enthusiastically and said they'd really have a go. This tape starts just as I began to explain the first warm-up exercise:

[*General murmur of conversation as people find a space on the floor of the hall.*]

A.P.: Right! If we could have a bit of hush we'll be able to get going. The first ...

PERCY: I hope that these activities are well-advised! I feel in my bones that I should be curled in a corner balancing the brim-full container of character until rehearsal commences.

THYNN: He means he's not sure if he's learned his lines yet. He wants to grab a chance to ...

PERCY: How dare you! I am word perfect! My method is ...

EDWIN: Let's get on, shall we? I'm sure Percy knows his lines, Leonard.

A.P.: Thank you, Edwin, thank you very much. Now, the first of our exercises is designed to help us to – *(reads from book)* 'loosen up and lose inhibitions'. So I want everybody to come up this end of the hall and stand with your backs against the wall so that we're all facing the door at the other end. Right, off you go!

[*Clatter and nervous murmur as all move.*]

A.P.: Shush, everybody! Now, this might seem a bit strange, but I want us all to ...

THYNN: Adrian?

A.P.: Yes, Leonard. What is it?

THYNN: Can I go to the toilet, please?

A.P.: Leonard, don't worry! I promise I won't make you do anything embarrassing – okay?

THYNN: We won't have to stand on boxes and do dances, or feel each other with blindfolds on or anything like that?

A.P.: No, nothing like that.

THYNN: Or one of us lie on the floor and the others stand round in a circle talking about him?

A.P.: No, Leonard!

GERALD: We *are* doing the one where we exchange clothes with the person we like least, while everyone watches, aren't we, dad?

THYNN: *(Panic stricken.)* I'm going to the boys' tiddler room!

A.P.: Come back, Leonard! Gerald was joking, *weren't* you, Gerald?

THYNN: *(Warily.)* Were you, Gerald?

GERALD: 'Course I was, Leonard. *(Blithely.)* Sorry, dad!

A.P.: If we were Russians, Gerald, I would be very tempted to show you where the crayfish spend the winter.

THYNN: Eh?

PERCY: I believe he meant ...

A.P.: Never mind what I meant! Let's get on. Now, for our first exercise we're all going to shout as loud as we can down the hall.

CHARLES: *(Nervously.)* Err ... ?

A.P.: Yes, Charles?

CHARLES: Err ... I'm not really just err ... clear about what we should err ... shout ...

A.P.: Well, the book suggests that everyone should shout, 'I hate you!' Sounds a bit funny, I know, but that's what it says. The idea is we clear out all the repressed aggression and bad temper that's got stuck inside and pushed down and err ... that sort of thing ...

[*Blank silence for a couple of seconds.*]

THYNN: I'm going to the boys' tiddl ...

A.P.: STAND STILL, LEONARD! No exercise – no uniform! Now, everybody, after three – one! two! thr ...

CHARLES: *(In an abrupt reedy scream.)* I hate you!

[*Shocked silence.*]

A.P.: Yes, Charles. Err ... good effort. If we could just try it together this time. Ready, everyone? One! Two! Three!

ALL: *(A pathetic, totally unaggressive mooing sound.)* I hate you ...

VERNON: ... in love.

A.P.: No, Vernon, we don't add 'in love', on the end. As for the rest of you, I don't honestly think an awful lot of aggression came out of us then, do you? Now come on, backs to the wall and really shout it out. After three again. One! Two! Three!

ALL: *(A faintly annoyed mooing sound.)* I hate you ...

CHARLES: In l ... sorry!

A.P.: Look, let's just try to imagine the person or thing we hate most, and then try again, right? Edwin, what would that be for you?

EDWIN: Hmmm ... interesting. I think for me it would be the devil.

[*Impressed murmur.*]

A.P.: Good! Stenneth, what about you? Who do you hate most?

STENNETH: *(With passion.)* Those who wantonly destroy balsa-wood models without compunction!

A.P.: Err ... yes, right – good one, Stenneth. Leonard, dare I ask?

THYNN: Me.

A.P.: Pardon.

THYNN: Me. I'm the one I hate most – especially when I'm drinking.

[*Embarrassed pause.*]

EDWIN: I don't hate you, Leonard – I love you. You're my friend. *(Slap of hand on shoulder.)* Charles, what about you? Who do you hate most?

CHARLES: *(Vaguely.)* Err ... Joe Bugner I think ...

A.P.: Why Joe Bugner?

CHARLES: I don't really know. I just really ...

PERCY: Loneliness! For me it is accursed loneliness! That I can shout at. Loneliness ...

A.P.: Well, I think we're really getting somewhere now. You see! Everyone's got something they'd like to have a shout at. Vernon, what's your pet hate?

VERNON: *(With wild intensity.)* I really hate it when you have a bath, then suddenly realise you've forgotten to bring a towel in, and you're staying in someone else's house, and you shout for someone to fetch one from your bedroom, then suddenly remember you've left your dirty old socks and a Biggles book lying around in your room and there's nothing else you can do and you want to die!

THYNN: Have you got *Biggles and the Little Green God,* Vernon? That's the only one I haven't ...

A.P.: Right, well I think that's everyone ...

THYNN: Expostulated Algy ...

A.P.: What?

THYNN: Opined Ginger ...

A.P.: Do be quiet, Leonard.

THYNN: Voiced Bertie ...

A.P.: Leonard!

THYNN: Encapsulated Biggles, as the air commodore pushed his cigarette box across the desk ...

A.P.: Leonard, be quiet! *(Pause.)* Thank you. Now, we've all identified something or someone that we hate – right?

GERALD: Daddy, dear!

A.P.: *(Sighing.)* Sorry, Gerald. I forgot you. What do you hate most?

GERALD: *(Pathetically.)* Being left out by daddy-doos, I think.

A.P.: If you don't want to be left out altogether by daddy-doos, you'd better decide what you really hate most, Gerald.

GERALD: What, seriously?

A.P.: *(A little taken aback.)* Well, err ... yes, seriously.

GERALD: *(After a short pause.)* Well, if you must know, I hate it when people think that just because I tell jokes and take the mickey sometimes it means I'm not serious about anything, or that I don't really believe in God, or that I'm just being nasty. I expect it's my fault sometimes, but ... well that's what I really hate most ...

A.P.: *(Quietly.)* Thank you, Gerald. *(Briskly.)* That's everyone, then. Let's ...

THYNN: Err ... excuse me, air-commodore?

A.P.: *(Testily.)* What now?

THYNN: You haven't told us what *you* hate most – interrogated Von Stalhein.

A.P.: Apart from ridiculous un-funny allusions to Biggles books, you mean?

THYNN: Sorry.

VERNON: Go on, Adrian, tell us who you hate most. We've all said ours, so it's sort of only really thingy, isn't it?

A.P.: Never let it be said that I am anything but thingy, Vernon! The thing I hate most, now let me see ... I think probably one of the things I hate most is anyone being nasty to Anne. I can't stand that. *(Ruefully.)* I'm the only one who's allowed to be nasty to Anne. I didn't mean that I never err ... you know. But I don't like it when someone else err ... isn't – or rather – is being err ... nasty.

EDWIN: I think that really is everyone now, Adrian.

A.P.: Good! Now, stand up straight – backs to the wall! After three. Think about all those things we've just said we hate so much! In fact, let's not shout '*I* hate you.' Let's shout '*We* hate you,' as loud as we can – really feel it together! Ready?

[*Chorus of agreement.*]

ALL: We hate you!

A.P.: Not bad! Not at all bad! But we can do even better! One, two, three!

ALL: *(With considerable volume.)* We hate you!!

A.P.: And again! Really let it go!

ALL: *(Quite caught up in it now.)* We hate you!!!

A.P.: One more time! One, two, three, go!!

ALL: *(A terrifying scream.)* WE HATE YOU!!!

[*Sound of a body slumping to the floor as* MRS FLUSHPOOL *collapses with the shock of seven people – including her husband – screaming hate at her as she comes in through the door at the opposite end of the hall.*)

A.P.: Oh, no! We were going to be specially ...

[*Clatter of feet as everyone surrounds* MRS F. *and helps her to her feet.*]

CHARLES: *(Wildly.)* I wasn't shouting at you – I was shouting at Joe Bugner!

MRS F.: *(Faintly.)* What?

EDWIN: It was just an unfortunate coincidence, Victoria. As far as I was concerned, I was shouting at the dev – err ... at somebody completely different. I do hope ...

VERNON: *(Comfortingly.)* It was in love ...

MRS F.: *(In high-pitched bewilderment.)* How can you scream at someone that you hate them *in love?*

VERNON: You don't understand, Mrs Flushpool. We were using our imaginations. I was pretending I'd got no clothes on.

MRS F.: An orgy! Stenneth, how could you?

STENNETH: *(Sounding like the captain of the Titanic surveying his future just after the impact.)* Victoria, words fail me ...

A.P.: It's actually very simple to explain, Victoria. We were doing an exercise from a drama book I've bought. You get rid of aggression and stuff by shouting 'I hate you' as loudly as you can. That's what we were doing. You just happened to come in when we reached our err ... peak, as it were. I'm awfully sorry. Please forgive us.

MRS F.: *(Graciously.)* In the natural you would certainly have found me intransigent. I hope that I am now capable of exercising reflective redemption.

THYNN: Yes, but are we forgiven?

EDWIN: That's what Victoria meant, Leonard.

STENNETH: So *I* am err … forgiven, Victoria?

MRS F.: Naturally, Stenneth. It is a scriptural obligation. I would, however, be extremely interested to know what your particular imaginary object of hatred happened to be.

STENNETH: *(The blood draining from his words.)* Of – of course, my dear. My err … main object of hatred was, well, it was actually err … it was … *(Looks imploringly at the the others.)* Henry the Eighth! Wasn't it, everybody?

EDWIN: Err … yes, I believe it was something like that, Stenneth, yes.

THYNN: *(Trying to be helpful.)* I thought it was Henry the Seventh …

A.P.: *(Firmly.)* It was Henry the Eighth, Leonard! Wasn't it, Gerald?

GERALD: Yes! Definitely! 'Enery the Eighth!

MRS F.: Very suitable I'm sure, Stenneth. A notorious bigamist.

A.P.: Perhaps if you're feeling okay now, Victoria, we could move on to the second exercise. What do you think?

MRS F.: That rather depends on what the second exercise *is*, Adrian. I will not wink at impropriety.

THYNN: Eh?

A.P.: It really is quite proper, Victoria. We simply sit in a circle and think peaceful thoughts, then share our mental images with others. It's the opposite of the first one if you like. Instead of thinking about the thing you hate most, you think about nice, beautiful things, things that make you feel happy and relaxed.

THYNN: *(Remembering the 'Be nice to MRS F.' vow and overdoing it as usual.)* Dear, sweet, kind Mrs Flushpool, do please be good enough to join us in this little tiny exercise. We shall be miserable and upset if your pretty face isn't there for all to see in our little circle in a moment.

MRS F.: *(Unexpectedly flattered by Thynn's nonsense.)* Well, of course, one wants to be co-operative. *(To A.P.)* You say we are to sit in a circle?

A.P.: Err ... yes, if we could all just form a rough circle on the floor ...

[*General commotion as everyone tries to form a circle. A minute passes.*]

EDWIN: I think that's about as near as we're going to get, Adrian – a sort of bulgy oval.

A.P.: Right, well, if we could all be quiet now, and just concentrate on something that makes us feel good ...

[*Brief silence, broken only by Thynn sighing heavily.*]

A.P.: Could we just err ... come back now, as it were? Any volunteers to start us off ... ?

CHARLES: I could just ...

A.P.: Okay, Charles, off you go.

CHARLES: Well, I just sort of pictured myself dying and being lifted up by two heavenly cherubims until I found that I had entered a city of gold, where I joined a white-robed throng singing praise and worship for all eternity to he who is above all and in all, and joy and elation filled the firmament!

A.P.: Wonderful! Leonard, what about you?

THYNN: *(Dreamily.)* I'm just starting my fifth pint of Theakston's Old Peculiar ...

A.P.: Ah, right ... err, Vernon?

VERNON: I was picturing a really huge auditorium full of people responding to a superb message from an internationally acclaimed evangelist and preacher.

A.P.: Who was the preacher?

VERNON: *(Modestly.)* Me.

[*Some laughter.*]

A.P.: No, no, fair enough. Better to be honest. Edwin? Were you imagining you were pope?

EDWIN: *(Laughing.)* I'm afraid mine was very boring. I was lying in the sun on a beautiful sandy beach, just listening to seagulls and seasidey sort of noises. Lovely. Not very holy I'm afraid ...

GERALD: Mine isn't, either. I was only a blue, a pink and a black away from a hundred and forty-seven break. Steve Davis was sitting on his chair looking as sick as an interesting pig. *(Sighs.)* It was wonderful!

A.P.: It was a blooming miracle, seeing as the highest break you've ever scored is seventeen!

GERALD: Oh, come off it, dad! When we played at Frank Braddock's club I scored twenty-five points, and it would have been thirty-two if I hadn't mis-cued on the next black.

A.P.: Twenty-five points, my aunt! You mis-cued after seventeen points. I remember it as clearly as anything.

GERALD: That's good, coming from you. You're the only person I know who chalks up *after* a mis-cue!

A.P.: Well, who pushed his cue up his own nose when he was breaking off and trying to look professional and cool?

GERALD: Well, who said, 'Aren't the webs a problem?' when he was told there was a swannecked spider on every table in the club?

A.P.: That was a joke, and you know it! I never thought ...

EDWIN: *(Breaking in diplomatically.)* Adrian, you haven't told us what your err ... beautiful thoughts were.

A.P.: What? Oh, right, sorry. Yes, err ... actually I was just blank really. Quite serene, but blank, void, one of those empty pockets of ...

GERALD: Now we're back to your snooker again.

A.P.: Sorry?

GERALD: Empty pockets ...

A.P.: Now look, if you think ...

STENNETH: *(Miles away, eyes still shut, suddenly speaks with a deep American accent.)* To boldly go where no man has gone before ... warp five if you please, Mr Sulu ... beam me up, Scotty ... what in hell's name *is* that, Mr Spock?

275

MRS F.: Stenneth!

STENNETH: *(Coming to with a start.)* Condition red! I mean err ... yes, Captain – I mean, yes, Victoria.

GERALD: We can't imagine what you were thinking about, Stenneth.

[*General laughter.*]

STENNETH: *(Rather embarrassed.)* It used to be my – my favourite programme you see. I suppose it seemed so wonderfully adventurous and exciting. You never quite knew what was going to happen next, whereas ...

MRS F.: Yes, Stenneth? Whereas what?

STENNETH: Whereas my own life *(hastily),* although satisfactory in many ways, was somewhat err ... predictable.

[*Pause as everyone waits for* MRS F. *to devour* STENNETH.]

MRS F.: *(Surprisingly subdued.)* I am aware, Stenneth, that your life is not, perhaps, as fulfilled and err ... pleasant as it might be. I am also aware that I am not guiltless in respect of your occasional – your continual lack of contentment. I have been attempting since I first ...

STENNETH: *(Genuinely distressed.)* Please, my dear, you mustn't ...

MRS F.: Since I first undertook this role as an – angel, I have been attempting to imagine myself as such a being – with little success I am afraid. Just now I was attempting to experience peace by picturing Stenneth and myself at our favourite places and activities – or rather, those activities that I assumed gave enjoyment to Stenneth despite never having asked him – and I was quite unable to properly relax. For some reason the challenge of having to present myself as an angel, a messenger from God, has made me realise something that I fear I have known for rather a long time. Namely, that, despite my redemption from the natural, I am consistently harsh and unpleasant to others, and – and I ... oh, dear ...

[*Sobs, sniffs and tissue-wielding sounds as* MRS F. *bursts into tears for the first time that any of us can remember.*]

STENNETH: Victoria, you're crying! Please don't cry, my dear ...

THYNN: *(Kindhearted but wildly misguided.)* Don't cry, Mrs Flushpool. We don't think you're any of those things you said. We think you're the nicest, kindest, most wonderful person in the whole church! We think ...

EDWIN: *(Taking over with that quiet authority he shows sometimes.)* No, Leonard – I know you're just trying to be kind, but that's not what's needed here. Victoria, you make me feel very humble. I only hope that I shall be able to reveal my negative side as openly as you have when my time comes. We forgive you fully for anything you've ever said or done that might have upset us, don't we, everybody?

[*Enthusiastic assent from all, especially Stenneth, nearly in tears himself.*]

EDWIN: And so will God, if we ask him. Do you want us to pray for a little while now before we go on with the rehearsal, Victoria?

MRS F.: *(Whispering.)* Yes, please – I would ...

EDWIN: Okay, we will. Loving heavenly father, we pray – Leonard, is your machine over there recording?

THYNN: Yes, it is. Do you want me to ... ?

EDWIN: Switch it off, there's a good chap.

[*Sound of footsteps, followed by a click! as the tape-recorder is switched off.*]

SIX

ANNE DOES THE TRICK

It was quite right of Edwin to tell Leonard to switch the tape-recorder off when we began praying with Victoria. It was better kept private. But no one remembered to switch it on again. I pretended to commiserate with Leonard when we realised that the whole of one rehearsal had gone unrecorded, but I was quite glad really. It wasn't the line learning. I was pleasantly surprised at how well everyone knew their words. Leonard was quite upset to find that he had hardly anything to do. We had a read-through first, which went very well. It was the next bit that got rather confusing. Perhaps I was trying to be just a fraction more professional than I really am. I wanted to use all the proper theatrical terms like they did in *The Third Book of Theatrical Themes for Theological Thespians,* but I made the mistake of not explaining them properly first. With my eyes fixed on a series of diagrams I'd drawn the night before, I called out such a complicated barrage of instructions that, at one point, everyone ended up in a bewildered huddle in one corner of the hall and got annoyed with me. Things got a lot easier after I explained what 'stage-left', and 'up-stage' and 'stage-right' and 'down-stage' actually mean. Percy already knew, of course, so did Gerald, but the others took some time to absorb it all. I was deeply thankful that Thynn wasn't part of the acting team. He has a great deal of trouble sorting out left and right at the best of times.

The lions were a bit feeble at first. Then Gerald suggested they should imagine they were sitting in church, and that George Farmer had just reached that point in one of his twelve fruit-gum talks, when, after forty-five minutes, he says, 'That's a very important point, and I want to examine it more fully later ...' After that they really put some aggression into their roaring. I had to stop Leonard roaring with them, but I sympathised – we all did.

Overall, the acting wasn't bad at all. Percy was a touch Knight-of-the-Theatre-ish, and Victoria tended to enter like the Fairy Godmother in Cinderella, but the standard seemed generally high, and by the time we finished everyone knew basically where to go and what to do. Gloria and Norma were there, sitting at the side and giggling when I got things wrong. Anne and Mrs Thynn came along later as well. Mrs Thynn assured me that she'd booked the lion costumes for our next rehearsal, and Norma was being very organised about all the other clothes, so that part of the arrangements seemed to be well looked after. Gloria said that the make-up was so simple that there was no point in doing it until the second rehearsal, which would have to be our dress-rehearsal as well. There was just one major problem. At the end of the rehearsal Anne came up and whispered the question that I'd been asking myself all evening: 'Darling, where on earth have Elsie and William got to?'

'I don't know!', I hissed, 'I wish I did. I asked Edwin where Elsie was earlier, but he said that as far as he knew they were coming. I could throttle her – fancy not coming at all!'

I grabbed Edwin just before he left, and asked him whether he was planning to quiz his daughter about what was going on, but he smiled and said, 'Adrian, I'm going to annoy her intensely by appearing totally unconcerned about her absence tonight. I think she ought to sort it out with you – or you and Anne, perhaps.'

Later that weekend I phoned Elsie and asked as casually as I could (bearing in mind that I actually wanted to explode at her) whether she was planning to come to next Friday's rehearsal. There was a short pause, then she said, 'I suppose so, yes.' Conquering a temptation to swear loudly, I asked her if she could come half an hour early so that we could have a chat. She said, even more reluctantly, 'I suppose we could if we must, yes.' I said thank you quite calmly, then went into the garden and beat the hedge with a stick for a while.

The next Friday I felt quite nervous. Thynn didn't help much by arriving at the hall three-quarters of an hour early with his ever-present machine, very excited about the dress-rehearsal and especially about trying on the soldier's uniform that Norma had promised to get for him. I told him he'd have to clear off while Anne and I spoke to Elsie and William, so, grumbling a bit, he went off to buy a peach, and pester George Farmer in his fruit shop round the corner.

It was probably a good idea of Anne's that she should speak to the young couple on her own. She said that with the play on my mind, and feeling as angry as I did, I would degenerate into my Basil Fawlty mode within two minutes of starting the conversation. Neither of us realised that Leonard had left his machine switched on before he went out. Obviously we would have turned it off if we'd realised. I was quite amazed when Elsie agreed to allow this next bit to be included for publication. She's a good girl at heart, though.

I've started the transcription from when I left the hall 'to do something', and Anne settled down in the corner with Elsie and a very uneasy looking William.

ANNE: Elsie and William, you know why Adrian asked you to come early, don't you?

ELSIE: *(Defiantly.)* No!

WILLIAM: I suppose it's about ...

ELSIE: William doesn't know why he did either.

ANNE: Is that right, William?

ELSIE: He doesn't ...

ANNE: You do want William to tell the truth, don't you, Elsie?

ELSIE: *(Sulkily.)* Of course I do – I'm a Christian.

ANNE: Well then, William?

WILLIAM: Well, err ... I suppose it's about why we didn't come along last Friday, is it?

[*Unconcerned sniff from Elsie.*]

ANNE: That's absolutely right. Adrian and all the others missed you ever so much on Friday evening. You're essential to the play and you just weren't there. We don't want to get angry

281

with you, we just want to understand. Did you feel upset by anything that Adrian or anyone else said to you?

ELSIE: I was a tiny bit upset that my poems were turned down flat without any reason being given, and I don't quite understand why I'm a boy in this play, but as I told Mr Plass the other day, I'm a Christian, so I forgive him.

ANNE: You do?

ELSIE: Of course. I'm a ...

ANNE: But that's not the reason you didn't come on Friday?

ELSIE: No, it's not. It's – tell Anne, William.

WILLIAM: *(Uncertainly.)* Yes, well, Elsie felt that ...

ELSIE: *We* felt!

WILLIAM: *We* felt that err ... well, that if it was meant to err ... be err ... well ...

ELSIE: *(After loud throat-clearing.)* We felt that if God wanted this play to be performed he'd make sure it was all right on the night, and that we were being led to use our faith to believe that what we did would be all right without us having to let him down by doing it in our own strength, and – and ...

WILLIAM: And there was a film on at the pictures that we'd been looking forward to, so ...

ELSIE: *(Hastily and rather redly.)* It wasn't because of that! That was just a – coincidence. *(With more confidence.)* William and I had a time of prayer after tea on Friday and we really felt it was really right not to go to the rehearsal, didn't we, William?

WILLIAM: *(Unhappily.)* Well, you felt it first, and then – then I err ... sort of did ... I suppose ... actually, I really wanted to go.

ANNE: To the rehearsal you mean?

WILLIAM: Yes, you see ...

ELSIE: William!

WILLIAM: *(Eyes-shining sort of voice.)* ... I don't know if Mr Plass mentioned it to you, but I've got one or two ideas about using smoke in this play. So, actually, I was quite keen to err ... be there, but ...

ANNE: But Elsie talked you out of it?

282

ELSIE: No, we *both* thought – I told you we had a prayer-time!

ANNE: Elsie, darling, do you remember when you were a very little girl and you had a yellow canary?

ELSIE: *(Surprised and not far away from tears.)* Yes ... he was called Sammy ...

ANNE: Do you remember when you went on holiday one summer, you came round to see me, and asked if I'd look after Sammy while you were away?

ELSIE: *(A small voice.)* Yes.

ANNE: You were very serious and very anxious, and you made me promise two or three times that I'd feed him every single day without fail until you came back. Remember, sweetheart?

ELSIE: Mmm, yes ...

ANNE: But I bet you prayed every night while you were away that I wouldn't forget. Eh?

ELSIE: Yes, I used to screw my eyes tight shut and say 'Please, please, please, God!'

ANNE: And how was he when you did come back?

ELSIE: Fine – all right. He was all right, Anne.

ANNE: You didn't expect God to feed him while you were away, did you, love?

ELSIE: 'Course not ...

ANNE: It's exactly the same with the play, Elsie. We've got to pray as if prayer's the only thing that works, and then work as if work's the only thing that works. I can't remember who said that, but I think it's true.

ELSIE: Mmm, well, perhaps ...

ANNE: In any case – let's be honest – that wasn't the real problem, was it?

ELSIE: *(Very quietly.)* What do you mean?

ANNE: Well, you say you've forgiven Adrian for the things you felt hurt by, but it doesn't work automatically when you're a Christian. You have to pray about it, think about it, do something about it, and really *feel* it. You're still quite angry about your poem not being used, and the other thing, aren't you?

ELSIE: Well ...

ANNE: Well?

ELSIE: Yes, I s'pose I am ... *(Suddenly passionate.)* I don't look like a boy! I don't, do I Anne?

ANNE: *(Laughing affectionately.)* No one ever said you did, Elsie! If you must know – the reason Adrian wanted you to be the servant was that he knew once you were involved you'd put all your enthusiasm into it. He just wanted you to be in it. As for looking like a boy – well, do you want to know what Adrian said to me when you started going out with Gerald that time?

ELSIE: *(Avidly interested.)* Don't mind ...

ANNE: He said, 'Trust Gerald to end up with a little cracker like that.'

ELSIE: *(Blushingly pleased.)* Did he really say that?

ANNE: Would I lie to you, Elsie?

ELSIE: *(Simply.)* No, Anne, you don't tell lies. *(Pause.)* Did he really say that?

WILLIAM: *(Inadvisedly incredulous.)* About Elsie?

ELSIE: William!

ANNE: And, let's face it, Elsie, you're not the only one who had an idea turned down, are you? There were Charles and Vernon and Percy and Leonard, and even Gerald – although I don't think he was very serious really.

[*Pause.*]

ELSIE: I've been a bit silly, haven't I?

ANNE: I think you owe William an apology, don't you? He would have been here on Friday if it hadn't been for you, Elsie, wouldn't he?

[*Longer pause.*]

ELSIE: *(Reluctantly but bravely.)* Sorry, William, I was silly.

WILLIAM: *(Cheerfully.)* Does this mean it's full-steam ahead with the old smoke?

[*Sounds of me coming in through the door, trying to look as if I haven't been eavesdropping.*]

ADRIAN: I'm back! Everyone okay?

[*Sound of Elsie coming over and kissing me on the cheek.*]

ADRIAN: *(Terminally taken aback.)* What was that for?

ELSIE: It was a kiss from a little cracker. I'm sorry I wasn't there on Friday, Mr Plass, so is William, although it wasn't all his fault. But he is sorry, aren't you, William?

WILLIAM: Eh? Oh, yes! Now, let's talk smoke ...

Anne certainly did the trick! Elsie couldn't have been more cheerful and enthusiastic than she was for the rest of that rehearsal. Just as well really; it was *very* hard work. Everyone came this time – the whole caboodle! There was Edwin and the rest of the actors, nervous but excited, Norma and Mrs Thynn complete with black clothes and lion costumes, Richard, fussing around with his cheque book asking about 'legitimately incurred expenses', and Gloria, armed with a box of make-up, towels, cleansing-cream and other intriguing tins and tubes. I felt quite nervous at the thought that this little crowd milling around noisily in the hall was relying on me to sort everything out. My confidence wasn't helped by the discovery, just as the last person had been made up and we were all ready to begin, that Thynn, after arriving three-quarters of an hour early, was now nowhere to be seen. He came rushing in after another five minutes (during which I didn't swear out loud because, as Elsie would say, I'm a Christian) clutching a big plastic bag full of George's apples, and shouting, 'Did you get my uniform, Norma?' You can trust Norma. Not only is she charming and pretty and, well ... that sort of thing, but she never forgets a promise. Within a few minutes Leonard emerged from our little improvised changing room wearing the white uniform and plumed helmet of what I guessed to be something like a nineteenth century French colonial officer. The ideal costume for a prompter! He was overjoyed with it, and said it was an even better uniform than the one that Miss Glanthorpe had given him to wear.

The lions really didn't look too bad at all. The costumes were head-pieces with lion-like cloaks rather than complete cover-all affairs, so they didn't look as silly as they might have done. I'd paid a visit to the phantom of the opera a few days previously and managed to extract a sullen promise that the lions wouldn't be lit very brightly. I felt quite optimistic really, and a little ashamed of my doubts about Mrs Thynn's reliability. She said that the man in the costume hire shop told her he was hardly ever asked for his three lion costumes, so she'd decided to take them back tomorrow and re-hire them next Friday morning ready for the performance. That would make it cheaper. Richard nodded approvingly. So, like an idiot, did I, failing completely to register the significance of what Leonard's mother had said. A week later I was to remember her words only too well ...

Meanwhile, the rehearsal started really well. They all seemed to be remembering lines and moves perfectly, until Percy's next to last speech in the final run-through.

PERCY: *(Sounding like a cross between Topol and Olivier.)* Servant of the living God ... *(Pause.)*

THYNN: *(His first prompt of the evening.)* Hear my anguish.

PERCY: *(Irritably.)* I didn't need prompting, Leonard! That was a dramatic pause – a *planned* dramatic pause! *(To A.P.)* I shall commence my speech once more.

A.P.: All right, Percy, that's fine. From 'Servant of the living God', everybody. Leonard, don't prompt unless people really need it, okay?

THYNN: Well ...

A.P.: Off you go, Percy.

PERCY: *(After throat-clearing.)* Servant of the living God, hear my anguish!

[*Loud crunching noise as Thynn bites into one of his apples.*]

ALL: Ssh! Be quiet! Quiet! etc.

PERCY: *(Put off by Thynn's thunderous crunching.)* Has he kept his hand upon you in your danger? *(Long pause)* Err ... *(Longer pause.)*

A.P.: Come on, Leonard! Prompt!

THYNN: *(After swallowing half an apple whole and nearly choking to death.)* Sorry! I thought it was another dramatic pause. Err ... where are we? Oh, yes, right, here we are, Percy.

Does your God have power to –

PERCY: MAY I start my speech again, IF you please?

A.P.: *(Exasperated.)* Yes, yes! Off you go!

[*Another loud crunch as* THYNN *foolishly bites into a second apple.*]

PERCY: *(Determined to get it right this time.)*
Servant of the living God, hear my anguish,

> Has he kept his hand upon you in your danger?
> Does your God have power to rescue you from
>   from danger?

Err ... prompt!

THYNN: Drmnl smrnker mm ...

PERCY: What?

THYNN: Danmnk sprklk mwe ...

PERCY: I can't understand a word you're saying, Thynn!

THYNN: Dnml ...

[*Sound of* RICHARD COOK *slapping* THYNN *suddenly and violently on the back, followed by cries of dismay and disgust as the members of the cast are showered with bits of half-chewed apple.*)

A.P.: Leonard, I think that, as a general rule, it's pretty safe to assume that apple-eating and prompting don't go together. What do you think?

THYNN: Err ... yes, you could be right ... *(coughing fit.)*

After that we got to the end of the run-through without any mishaps, and I got everyone to sit round in a circle for a last chat before we all went home. It said in *The Third Book of Theatrical Themes for Theological Thespians* that there was no point in saying anything that might lower confidence, so I was determined to be positive at all costs.

[*Hubbub of excited conversation.*]

A.P.: Right! If we could have a bit of hush ...

[*Hubbub dies down gradually.*]

EDWIN: Shush, everybody! Adrian wants to talk to us.

A.P.: Thanks, Edwin. Err ... all I really want to say is that you've all done amazingly well. I can't believe it's this good after just two rehearsals. Well done! I don't just mean the acting. I mean the costumes and the make-up and ...

THYNN: The prompting.

A.P.: And the err … prompting, yes. Now, I've said all I want to say during the course of the evening, so it's over to you. Are there any questions?

MRS T.: We're *all* Christians, yer great goop!

THYNN: QUESTIONS, MOTHER!! ARE THERE ANY QUESTIONS!!

STENNETH: Err … I have a question.

A.P.: Yes, Stenneth?

STENNETH: I just wondered if it might be possible to keep our costumes when the production is over. I must confess I rather enjoy being a – a lion …

GERALD: Heh, good wheeze, Stenners! We could both roam the streets at night terrorising the locals with our bloodthirsty roars! What d'you say? We could eat Christians in the shopping precinct and …

A.P.: Thank you, Gerald. I'm sorry, Stenneth, but the costumes are only hired. I suppose you could always buy one if you wanted to err … use it at home.

GLORIA: I've got a leopard skin leotard at home, Stenneth, darling. We could get together and …

MRS F.: Err … could I just enquire, Adrian, whether you think my portrayal as err … an – an angel is, more or less err … satisfactory, or …

[*Amazing chorus of approval and praise from everyone else in the circle.*]

A.P.: Well, there's your answer, Victoria.

STENNETH: You're getting more like an angel every day, my dear, if I may say so.

NORMA: I agree, Victoria. It's been really lovely being with you this evening. You seem so sweet and relaxed.

THYNN: *(Goofily tactless.)* For a change.

[*Chorus of disapproval directed towards* THYNN *by everyone else in the circle.*]

289

MRS F.: No, no, Leonard is simply adhering to the truth. I do feel somehow – different. Perhaps there was more of the natural lodged in my personality than I realised ...

ANNE: You *are* different, Victoria, and it's lovely. Something else, Adrian – what about William's smoke? We haven't actually seen any of it yet, have we?

WILLIAM: Ah, yes, well ...

A.P.: William's going to – Carry on, William, you say.

WILLIAM: Adrian and I have agreed on a few places

A.P.: *Two* places!

WILLIAM: Err ... yes, two places where loads of smoke ...

A.P.: A *moderate* amount of smoke!

WILLIAM: Two places where a moderate amount of smoke would look really great!

PERCY: I hope that this smoke will not obscure any principal err ... characters. Where are these two places?

WILLIAM: Well, one is ...

A.P.: Nobody's going to be obscured, Percy. The first bit is just after Gerald's opening speech when we see the lions for the first time, and the second one is after Victoria's angel speech, just before everything goes dark. Okay?

PERCY: That sounds reasonably satisfactory. I trust, by the way, that my performance was of a sufficiently high standard?

ANNE: *(Sensing the worry beneath Percy's casual question.)* Percy, you were quite as wonderful as I always thought you'd be. Your King Darius is a *real* king!

GLORIA: You're *marvellous,* Percy darling! Scrumptious! I could eat you!

VERNON: Yes, Charles and I think you're really great, Mr Brain!

CHARLES: Yes, just sort of really ...

PERCY: *(Inflated beyond description now.)* Leonard? What do you think of my performance?

THYNN: Gorgeous, Percy, darling! Absolutely scrumptious! What do you think of my prompting, sweetheart?

[*Much amusement.*]

290

PERCY: *(Haughtily.)* Your prompting is singular, Leonard. I think that is the appropriate term – singular!

THYNN: Thank you, Percival. Wait a minute – what does singular mean?

A.P.: It means wonderful! Richard, are you happy with the way the money's going?

RICHARD: Our financial status is more than satisfactory, I'm very pleased to report. We are err ... several aardvarks in hand, as it were.

GERALD: *(Who wasn't at the meeting where Richard revealed his dream.)* Several aardvarks in hand? Is this a new currency they introduced in the middle of the night when I wasn't looking? Let me guess how it goes:

Six wombats equal one aardvark.

Two aardvarks equal one wolverine.

Three wolverines equal one yak.

Five yaks equal one hairy mammoth.

Got change for a gibbon, dad? I need a jerbil for the coffee machine. I reckon ...

A.P.: Gerald, Richard was making a little joke about ...

CHARLES: *(Astonished.)* Did you really make a joke, Father?

RICHARD: I was making a light-hearted reference to a prophetic dream vouchsafed to me recently in connection with the financial arrangements pertaining to this production.

GERALD: *(Genuinely bewildered.)* About aardvarks?

RICHARD: Yes, I saw, as it were, a mighty herd of ...

THYNN: Singular means only one, doesn't it? Very observant of you to notice there's only one of me, Percy. Well spotted!

PERCY: I did *not* mean that. I meant ...

GERALD: What were they doing, Richard?

RICHARD: *(Solemnly.)* Flying in formation.

PERCY: I meant, Leonard, if you must know, that your so-called prompting was execrable.

THYNN: Well, that's all right then!

[*Laughter.*]

291

GERALD: Tell us all about the aardvarks, Richard.

A.P.: *(Hastily.)* I think we're getting a bit off the point, aren't we? Are there any more questions in connection with the play?

ANNE: I'm sure we're all praying in a general sort of way about what happens next Friday evening, darling, but I wondered if it would be a good idea if Edwin just said a little prayer before we break up tonight.

A.P.: Sounds good to me. What does everyone else think?

ALL: Yes/Good idea/Mmm/Go for it, Edwin etc.

EDWIN: Okay – let's pray. *(Pauses.)* Dear Lord, I'm not much like Daniel – don't know how I'd get on with the lions, probably get eaten up, but I love you and I'd try to trust you. That's what I hope we all do next Friday – love you and try to trust you. We don't really know what success means, except that it's what you want. Look after us, Lord, keep us loving you and each other, and thanks for everything, past, present and future. In Jesus' name.

ALL: Amen.

[*Click! as Thynn switches his machine off.*]

SEVEN

LOVE A DUCK!

I didn't sleep much during the week leading up to the performance. Every night I lay awake imagining all the things that could possibly go wrong with 'Daniel in the Den'. On the Wednesday night I dreamed that Percy Brain dressed in a leopardskin leotard, and leading a pink aardvark on a chain, walked on to the stage, only to be crushed by a giant apple dropped by Thynn from somewhere up among the lighting bars. Turning to see what my neighbour in the audience thought about this, I found that I was sitting next to a King Penguin in evening dress who asked if he could borrow my feet. Then I woke up ...

By Friday evening my nerves were so bad that Anne suggested I should ask Edwin to take charge backstage, so that, apart from going round to wish everybody good luck, I could just take my place with Anne in the audience and watch from the front. It was a good idea. Edwin never flaps. He seemed quite happy to take on this role when I phoned him, so that's the way we arranged it.

There were eight entries in the festival competition, four scheduled to appear before the interval, and four after. Ours was the one due immediately after the interval. The hall was packed by seven-twenty. Eight local churches were heavily represented, as well as the usual crowd come out of interest or curiosity. At the back, seated behind a highly complex-looking control panel, sat the phantom of the opera surrounded by pieces of paper and sound cassettes. Somewhere among all that lot – I assumed – were our lighting requirements and a tape of lion roars, imitated with surprising success by William blowing through the outer covering of a matchbox.

At seven-twenty-eight Thynn emerged from the side door that led to the back-stage area, hurriedly scooped up a large china giraffe from a seat on the front row, and disappeared through the door again, much to the bewilderment of the giraffe's near-neighbours who'd been discussing its presence with great animation. At about seven-thirty-five, as the last few people straggled in and took their seats, the lights dimmed and Mr Lamberton-Pincney, who runs a group called 'Spot it and Stop it' in our church, stepped forward to begin his duties as Master of Ceremonies for the evening. I don't know how I sat still for that first half. The four offerings were worthy but dull, and seemed to go on for weeks. There wasn't a hint of humour in any of them – lots of death and repentance, and oodles of sad realisation. Ours wasn't a comedy either, of course, but at least there was a bit of drama and passion in it – and smoke! William was poised at the side of the phantom of the opera, ready for action when the time came. I began to feel quite hopeful.

At half-time the audience rose gratefully to pursue tea and biscuits, while I made my way backstage to see how everyone was getting on. They were all in one of the changing rooms, standing or sitting very tensely as though waiting for something. Thynn's machine was switched on.

[*Sound of door opening and closing as* A.P. *enters. Buzz of conversation stops abruptly.*]

A.P.: (*Brittle but bright.*) Hi, all! Everything okay?

VERNON: We've got a ...

EDWIN: Everyone's made up who needs to be, Adrian. Gloria's done a great job, so that's all right. Gerald and Percy and Elsie and Victoria and I have all got our gear on, as you can see, and good old Leonard's all dressed up ready for the prompting, so we're ready to go just as soon as ...

A.P.: (*Sensing disaster.*) As soon as what? What's gone wrong? Tell me!

[*Absolute uproar as everyone tries to speak at once.*]

EDWIN: (*Shouting.*) QUIET!

[*Silence.*]

A.P.: *(Tensely.)* Just tell me, Edwin – please!

EDWIN: It's just that – well, I might as well come straight out with it – the lion costumes haven't arrived yet.

A.P.: What?! Not arrived? They must have ...

THYNN: Mother hasn't ...

A.P.: Mother hasn't *what*? Somebody tell me!

[*More general uproar.*]

EDWIN: QUIET!!

[*Silence.*]

A.P.: Well?

EDWIN: Mrs Thynn hasn't arrived with the lion costumes yet. We've been waiting and waiting, thinking she'd turn up at any moment, but – well, I just don't know ...

A.P.: But ...

THYNN: She went into town this morning to do some shopping and get the costumes and things, and she said she'd see me at the hall this evening. I don't know where she is! I don't know what's happened to her! I don't know ...

GLORIA: *(At her best.)* All right, Leonard, calm down now. It's all going to be okay. Come to Auntie Gloria ...

CHARLES: Vernon's sort of just waiting ...

EDWIN: I've sent Vernon out to wait by the back door so he can let us know if – I mean – *when* she appears.

A.P.: *(Panicking wildly.)* But there's only a few minutes before we're on! What do we do without lions? We can't go on with the play if ...

[*Sound of door crashing open.*]

VERNON: She's coming!

[*Cries of relief and excitement.*]

GERALD: What about the costumes, Vernon?

VERNON: She's got a bundle under her arm. That must be them.

A.P.: Thank goodness for that! Do you want me to stay and ...

EDWIN: *(Shooing me out.)* No, no, we'll be fine. You go back and sit out front. We'll sort it all out. Off you go! Relax and enjoy the show.

A.P.: Well, if you're sure ...

EDWIN: Quite sure!

A.P.: *(At the door.)* Right, well, good luck, everyone! Good luck with the prompting, Leonard – and the recording.

THYNN: Yep! I'm going to switch it off now to make sure there's enough tape to record the actual ...

[Click! as Thynn switches off.]

I can't describe the relief I felt as I went back to my seat and told Anne what had happened.

'Just think,' I said, 'after all this work, how close we came to disaster.'

'Yes, darling,' she replied, handing me a cold cup of tea, 'I'm sure we'll be okay now. It's very exciting, isn't it? All these people watching!'

It *was* exciting. As people started filing back to their seats I felt quite shivery with anticipation. It was when all but one or two of the audience were settled in their places, that Richard Cook suddenly appeared through the door I'd closed, rushed up to me, knelt by my chair and started whispering urgently in my ear.

'Edwin sent me to say that Mrs Thynn's brought the costumes!'

'I knew that!' I hissed back. 'You didn't have to come and tell me that!'

'Yes, but she hasn't brought the right costumes!'

'Well, it's too late to worry about that. Leopards, tigers, whatever they are, you'll just have to go ahead.'

'But you don't understand! Percy and Gerald are already up on stage behind the curtain and they don't know that the costumes are ...'

'Richard, the lights are going down. Mr Lamberton-Pincney will be introducing our play any second now! They'll just have to go ahead, understand?'

'Yes, but ...'

'It's too late to worry, Richard!'

'But ...'

'Sssh!'

As Richard scuttled off worriedly towards the connecting door, the auditorium lights dimmed once more, and Mr Lamberton-Pincney's mournful, horse-like face was lit up by a spotlight shining on the curtains at the centre of the stage. In miserable, measured tones, he praised the offerings of the first half, and introduced the first play in the second part of the evening.

'Ladies and Gentlemen – Daniel in the Den!' As the curtains parted to reveal Percy standing majestically centre-stage, I felt a stab of pride and pleasure. He took two steps forward, moved a yard or two stage-right, then faced the audience and spoke in ringing tones. By now, Leonard had his recorder in position next to him, so the rest of the performance survives for posterity.

[*Sound of Percy's feet on the boards as he moves stage-right.*]

PERCY: Though ruling, ruled by men with hooded faces,
   Jealous, not for me, but for their honoured places.
   Lions indeed, made vicious not by hunger's pain,
   But by their lust for power and selfish gain.
   No darker hour than when I lightly penned
   This blind agreement to destroy my servant-friend.
   Within the veil of vanity my foolish eyes,
   Perceived my greatness, but could not perceive
     their lies.
   Oh, God of Daniel, guard your son tonight,
   Do not defend the law, defend the right.
   No sleep for me, no calm, no peace, no rest,
   For I have sanctified the worst, and sacrificed the best.

GERALD: *(Entering stage-left)*
   Pain is sharper than remorse,
   Death more final than regret,
   Darius will mourn tonight,
   But live his life, perhaps forget
   While Daniel faces fearful hurt,
   Beneath the dark remorseless flood
   That ... err ...

THYNN: *(Prompting perfectly.)* That flood of fear ...

GERALD: That flood of fear which runs before
The tearing down of flesh and blood.

It was marvellous! The opening speeches had been superb, despite Gerald's lapse of memory, which, thanks to Thynn, was hardly noticed. Now it was time for William's first opportunity to use his beloved smoke-machine. And he certainly used it! Despite my constant pleas for moderation, within two minutes the stage was completely filled with thick, impenetrable, yellow smoke. Percy and Gerald, their backs to the audience, peered hopelessly into the swirling mist, waiting for the lions to appear. The moment when the smoke cleared at last, and three large pantomime ducks waddled forward from the back of the stage will stay in my memory until the day I die. Percy was completely transfixed. From my place at the end of a row I could see his jaw hanging slackly down, his eyes wide and staring as the absurdly costumed trio tried to look menacing. A ripple of laughter passed through the audience as the ducks first hove into view, building to loud, uncontrollable guffaws, as they started to growl softly.

Gerald recovered first. Turning back towards the audience he gathered himself together, and delivered the following on-the-spot adaptation of his second speech.

GERALD: Down in the den where it's dark and black,
Where the lost men scream and the ducks go quack
Where a man whose gods are life and breath,
Will lose his gods in the beak of death.

[*Shouts of laughter.*]

Where the weak will lose their sworn religion,
In the tearing grip of a pin-tailed widgeon.

[*Screams of laughter.*]

THYNN: *(Audible to the mike, but not the audience.)* That's not what it says here!

PERCY: *(Recovering like the old trouper he is.)*
Oh, Daniel, Daniel save me from my madness,
Pray your God's compassion on my sadness,
Bid him send an all-forgiving rain,
To wash these excess mallards down the drain.

ELSIE: *(Entering stage left and getting the idea immediately.)*
I wait upon you master as you bade me wait,
To bring intelligence of Daniel and his fate.
Some moments past your man, of whom you're fond,
Was taken out and thrown into the pond.

PERCY: Save him God, hear my appeal!
Save him for that flock of teal!

THYNN: *(Louder.)* That's not what it says here! *(Wanders out onto the stage absent-mindedly, studying his script.)* That's not what it says here, Percy! There's nothing about ducks!

[*Wild laughter from the audience on seeing someone in a nineteenth-century French colonial officer's uniform wandering inexplicably around the stage among the ducks.*]

STENNETH: *(A muffled bleat through his duck head.)* She brought the wrong costumes, Leonard! She brought ducks!

GERALD: *(Pushing between STENNETH DUCK and THYNN to address the audience.)*
> Now the moment, now the test,
> See Jehovah's servant blessed,
> Standing here with troubled scowl
> Before these deadly water-fowl.
> Glad to earn the highest crown,
> By ending up in eiderdown.

[*Loud roars from the speakers as the 'phantom' puts on William's tape. Audience collapses again as the ducks bob up and down, opening and shutting their beaks in time with the roars.*]

THYNN: *(Wildly at centre-stage.)* You're all getting it wrong! There aren't any ducks in it!

EDWIN: *(Entering stage-left.)*
> Though I may be short of pluck
> I'm not afraid to face a duck!
> I'll cut these creatures into thirds,
> The stupid geriatric birds!

THYNN: *(Very indignant.)* That's *completely* wrong!

MRS F.: *(Entering stage-right with a very straight, severe face. Touches each duck's head in turn with her hand.)*
> Here they lie, those mighty killers,
> Harmless where great harm has been,
> Sleep, and when the dawn has risen,
> Tell the king what you have seen.

(Moves over and touches Edwin's head with her hand.)

Daniel, you *shall* go to the ball!

[*MRS FLUSHPOOL'S face suddenly cracks into a real smile and she laughs until she cries.*]

THYNN: *(Resting his arm on VERNON DUCK'S shoulder.)* Now that *is* wrong!

GERALD: If you would score, you mighty kings,
        Be sure, don't trust to luck.
        If you don't score by God's own law,
        You'll end up with a duck.

THYNN: That's not ... !

GERALD: Come on, everyone!

[*Gerald gets all on stage into a chorus line, and leads them into song.*]

ALL: Knees up Daniel Brown!
        Knees up Daniel Brown!
        Knees up! Knees up!
        Better get your knees up,
        Knees up Daniel Brown! Oi!

THYNN: We never sung that at rehearsals ...

At this point the phantom of the opera, knowing that he was supposed to black out the stage somewhere in the course of the action, decided that now would be as good a time as any. Who can blame him?

When the lights came back on, the cast of 'Daniel in the Ducks' Den' received the only standing ovation ever witnessed in that building. People cheered and clapped for a good three or four minutes, while the actors waved and bowed extravagantly until the applause died down. Thynn, postponing his quest for some basic understanding of what was going on, waved and bowed with the rest, a blank but happy grin stretched across his face.

I felt sorry for the people in the three plays that came after ours. Two of them were quite good, but there was no doubt about it – nothing, on this particular night, was going to match the emergence of those three ducks from the middle of William's smoke. I think I had experienced every emotion known to man during the 'Daniel' performance, and as I joined in the applause for the final offering of the evening I felt quite exhausted. Four more significant things were yet to happen, though, before we left for home that night.

First, Mr Lamberton-Pincney announced immediately after the final play had finished that the judges' overwhelming and unanimous decision was that 'Daniel in the Den' was the winning entry, and I was called up on stage to collect the little silver cup on behalf of our church, for a 'hilarious and cleverly devised comedy'. Feeling terribly guilty, I tried to explain to Mr Lamberton-Pincney and the audience that our play was meant to be serious and had only become funny by accident. The more I tried to explain, though, the more they obviously thought I was being terribly witty. They just laughed and clapped. In the end I gave up, and decided to explain to whoever was in charge later on.

The next thing was that Anne, who'd nearly died of laughing from 'ducks' onwards, steered me through the crowds of lingering theatre-goers to where a little old lady was sitting next to Leonard, still in his uniform and clutching Mr Hurd. They were chatting away like mad.

'Miss Glanthorpe,' whispered Anne in my ear. 'A little surprise I organised. Found her in the book. She's eighty-two!'

I looked at Anne for a moment, then moved closer to eavesdrop.

'You were absolutely marvellous, Leonard,' Miss Glanthorpe was saying, her little eyes twinkling as she surveyed the white-clad figure.

Leonard beamed happily.

'I don't quite understand though,' went on the old lady, 'the significance of this splendid uniform, and I was just wondering why you have that big china giraffe sitting on your knee ...'

'Oh, that's easy to explain,' said Leonard confidently, 'I was wearing uniform because I was the prompter, and I was supposed to stay out of sight so that the giraffe couldn't see me when Percy Brain forgot his lines.'

'I see, dear. How silly of me to be so dense.' The little eyes twinkled even more. 'You know, Leonard ... ?'

'Yes, Miss Glanthorpe?'

'You really haven't changed at all ...'

The third thing was that as we moved away towards the backstage area we almost collided with Frank Braddock, our neighbour, and author of the play we'd just mangled. He was with

302

Father John, an old friend of his, and an occasional very welcome guest speaker at our church.

'Frank,' I said apologetically, 'I just don't know what to say. I'm so ...'

'Don't apologise!' boomed Frank taking his unlit pipe out of his mouth. 'I was just saying to old Bungles here that I haven't enjoyed anything so much in years. The moment when old Thynn wandered on in his uniform was just – I dunno, I could've died! My version was much more boring than yours.'

'It's nice of you to say that, Frank,' I replied gratefully, 'but it wasn't exactly what I set out to do. Winning was an accident. I can't really see this evening as a success, not really.'

'Not a success?' Father John broke in gently. 'Adrian, I've never seen Victoria Flushpool as she was on that stage this evening. Her eyes shone, she was laughing, she was part of you all. She's different. I wouldn't be at all surprised if the experience of rubbing up against each other in a real, side-by-side effort like this had changed all of you in one way or another. It all depends whose success you're talking about, you know. I sometimes think that football teams and dramatic societies might be just as important as prayer-meetings and Bible-studies ...'

'Come on, Bungles!' Frank slapped his friend on the back. 'Enough deep stuff! We've just got time for a pint if we're quick ...'

The fourth and last thing to happen was finding the cast and crew of 'Daniel in the Den', still sitting in the changing room behind the stage. Thynn followed Anne and me through the door as we went in, and stood leaning against the wall cuddling his giraffe. All conversation stopped as soon as I appeared, and they all stared at me, waiting to see what I'd say. I thought of what Father John had said as I looked round at the familiar faces. Vernon and Charles, as earnest as ever, had little frowns beneath hair still lank from being enclosed in hot costumes. Victoria and Stenneth were sitting closer together than usual – they seemed lighter somehow. Gerald looked the same as ever, leaning on the radiator and giving me a little quizzical smile. I suddenly realised how grown up he was getting. Richard was sitting on an old, burst horse-hair sofa, jammed in tightly by Gloria on one side and Norma on the other. William and Elsie sat cross-legged on the floor gazing up at me. They looked even younger than usual. Percy was in the only armchair, legs crossed stylishly, head thrown back, but watching me with wide eyes. Mrs Thynn was doing something busily with a piece of cloth held in her fingers. Her eyes darted up to meet mine every few seconds. Edwin was standing by the window looking as serene as ever. Anne stood very still beside me. There was someone else there as well, right in the middle of us, the one who decides what success really means.

'Those ducks!' I said, and we all burst into laughter at the same moment.